Introduction	2-5
How to use this guide	6-7
Subject index	8-10
Facilities for disabled people	15
England	17-59
Something's brewing	24-25
Heard on the grapevine	36-37
Going to pot	48-49
Whisky galore	60
Scotland	61-71
Breathing life into glass	72-73
Wales	75-81
Power to the people	82-83
Northern Ireland	85-89
Farming through the seasons	90-91
Further information	92-109
Index of advertisers	110-112

ENGLAND

SCOTLAND

WALES

N. IRELAND

Visit Britain at Work

There's a special kind of magic about watching people at work and seeing things being made. This guide is all about places you can visit where you can do just that. They range from the traditional to hi-tech, from tiny one-man operations to giant industrial installations.

SO MUCH TO SEE

You'll find lots of great ideas for visits in this guide, and there's something to be found in practically every part of the country. Often these reflect local specialities you'll find nowhere else — like Scotch whisky distilleries or the famous potteries of the English Midlands. Some might be surprisingly close to home, ideal for a day out with

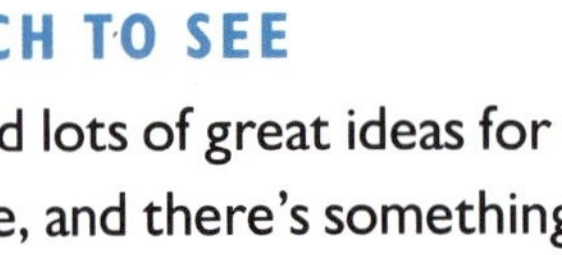

the family or for a group or school party visit. A great many others are to be found in Britain's holiday regions, and it's a good idea to have your copy with you whenever you go away — you never know when you might have an afternoon to spare. Remember that many places will be open all year round, so they're well worth seeking out if you're taking an early or late-season break.

THE FIRST OF ITS KIND

The idea for *Visit Britain at Work* grew out of a government initiative — enthusiastically supported by the CBI — aimed at encouraging Britain's industrial and craft companies to open their doors to the visitor. It is the first fully comprehensive official guide to this new and fast-developing area of tourism ever to be published.

All shapes and sizes

You'll be amazed at just how broad is the selection of places covered in *Visit Britain at Work*. There are the long-established favourites you'd expect — the potters and weavers, the breweries and distilleries. But there are also many listings that might be totally new to you, ranging in scope from herb growers to the mighty Channel Tunnel project. Some have already established a long-standing reputation as visitor attractions, while others have opened their doors to the public this year for the very first time.

SEE FOR YOURSELF

Whatever the size and scope of their operations, all the owners whose companies are listed here have a single clear idea in mind — that you should learn a little bit more about who they are and what they do. Some of their names, and the goods they produce, might be very familiar to you. Others you might never have heard of until now — and yet it's surprising, however well you think you know an area, what you might have overlooked. Without *Visit Britain at Work* you

might never have known about the vineyard on the other side of the hill to your holiday cottage, or that visitors (and children especially) are welcome to look round that picturesque farm you've passed dozens of times on your travels.

THE BUTCHER, THE BAKER . . .

As you'll have gathered, there's a fantastic range of crafts and industries to be found in these pages (and yes, there really is a candlestick maker). In some of them history plays its rightful part but the overwhelming emphasis is on the here and now. Often there's a strong bias towards a hands-on approach, because finding out how things are done at first hand is a fascinating and very valuable experience, especially for youngsters. That's why so many of the entries will be of interest not just for holiday visitors, but for schools and other organisations as well. Party rates are often available and special facilities might well be possible. So if you see something that interests you, ring or write directly — you'll find phone numbers and addresses in each entry. The most popular places to visit sometimes have a habit of booking up remarkably quickly, so to avoid disappointment it pays to be fast off the mark . . .

How to use this Guide

Visit Britain at Work has been designed to be as easy to use as possible. It's arranged in four see-at-a-glance sections covering in turn England, Scotland, Wales and Northern Ireland. Choose where you want to go first, and then see what's on offer. Each region is broken down county by county and town by town, with each establishment pinpointed alphabetically by name. If you're looking for something specific, such as a slate mine or a silk mill, then simply look it up in the subject index provided. What could be more comprehensive and yet, at the same time, so wonderfully straightforward?

WHAT'S AVAILABLE?

Every company listed here has made a special effort to make visitors welcome. Facilities naturally vary, though as much information as possible is given in each entry on these pages — including the all-important details like opening times, parking facilities and directions for how to get there. As you'll see, many places lay on guided tours so you can be personally shown everything that's going on. This is frequently supplemented by practical demonstrations and/or audio-visual and video presentations. Don't be afraid to ask questions — you might even be invited to try your hand yourself! It's quite likely that afterwards you'll be able to buy samples of what you've seen being made, and to have a drink or a bite to eat. A simple code of symbols (see the opposite page) shows you exactly what to expect.

PLANNING AHEAD

Many places do not require an advance booking but in some cases it is essential, however, you'll see the name of the person to contact. There may also be limitations on the size of parties. Wherever possible every effort has been made to accommodate disabled visitors but sometimes, unfortunately, suitable facilities may not be available, simply because of the nature of the work undertaken.

NEW IDEAS & PLACES

We find it very helpful to receive comments from readers about establishments they have visited and which they feel should be included in the guide. We would like to hear from you. Please mention this guide when booking or visiting establishments.

NEW LONDON DIALLING CODES

Please note that from 6th May 1990 the 01- telephone number prefix will change to 071-for inner London and 081-for outer London respectively.

EXPLANATION OF SYMBOLS

(50)	Parking facilities for cars. Number of spaces shown in brackets
CP	Coach parking facilities
D	Suitable facilities for disabled people (see page 15 for further details)
V	Visitor centre or room
R	Restaurant
SB	Snack bar/vending machine
S	Shop or products for sale

Subject index

A

Aircraft/aviation
Fleet Air Arm Museum **47**

B

Bakeries
Warburtons Ltd **40**

Bellfoundry
John Taylor Bellfoundry & Museum **41**

Bobbin making
Stott Park Bobbin Mill **27**

Breweries
Bass Museum, Visitor Centre and Shire Horse Stables **47**
Bass Mitchells & Butlers Ltd **55**
Eldridge Pope & Co Ltd **30**
Frederic Robinson Ltd **22**
Whitbread Beer Co(Magor)**78**
Whitbread & Company plc (Hartlepool) **22**
Whitbread & Company plc (Preston) **41**

Brick & tile making
Bulmer Brick & Tile Co Ltd **53**

Bridges
Tower Bridge **43**

Bronzes
Heredities Ltd **26**

C

Candle-making
Colonial Candle Co Ltd **27**

Cashmere products & textiles
James Johnston & Co of Elgin Ltd **68**

Chocolate/confectionery
Cadbury World **55**

Cider farm/making
Callestock Cider Farm **23**
James White Suffolk Cider **52**
Merrydown Wine plc **55**

Clog making
Maude Walkley Clogs **57**

Coal mining
Scottish Mining Museum **68**
Yorkshire Mining Museum **58**

Cookery
Tilbec **33**

Cotton Mill
Quarry Bank Mill **22**

Craft workshops/centres
Bosham Walk Craft Centre **54**
Dean Heritage Centre **32**
Norfolk Rural Life Museum **45**
Lathkill Dale Craft Centre **27**
Norselands Gallery Studio Two **46**
Ridgeway Cottage Industry Centre **28**
Stockford Craft Museum **20**

D

Diamonds
London Diamond Centre **42**

Docklands
London Docklands Development Corp **42**

E

Enamels
Staffordshire Enamels Ltd **51**

F

Farm, country parks & dairies
Easton Farm Park **53**
Farm and Country Visits **54**
Longdown Dairy Farm **34**
Nevern Dairies Ltd **78**
Park Lodge Farm Centre **44**
Redesdale Dairy **46**
Sacrewell Farm & Country Centre **21**
South Leaze Sheep Farm **56**
Tattenhall Dairy Products Ltd **21**

Fishing tackle
House of Hardy Ltd **45**

Flint mill
Cheddleton Flint Mill **50**
Etruria Industrial Museum **50**

Flood barrier
Thames Barrier Visitors Centre **43**

Flour Mills
Lower City Mills **70**
Otterton Mill Ltd **29**
John Ridley Projects Ltd **69**

Flowers
Winter Flora Ltd **52**

Furniture
Redman & Hales Ltd **31**
Treske Limited **58**

G

Glassware
Caithness Crystal Ltd (King's Lynn) **45**
Caithness Glass plc (Wick) **66**
Caithness Glass plc (Perth) **70**
Coloroll Edinburgh Crystal **67**
Dartington Crystal **29**
Oban Glassworks **64**
Royal Brierley Crystal **56**
Tutbury Crystal Glass Ltd **50**
Tyrone Crystal **88**

H

Herbs
Scotherbs **69**

Heritage centre
Port Sunlight Heritage Ctr **44**

Honey farm
Quince Honey Farm **30**

Horse Racing
Lambourn Trainers Assoc **20**
Newmarket Equine Tours **53**

I

Industrial museum/heritage
Kelham Island Industrial Museum **57**
Summerlee Heritage Trust **67**

Insurance
Lloyd's of London **41**

J

Jewellery making
Hebridean Jewellery **71**

L

Leather making
Walsall Leather Centre Museum **56**

M

Mineral quarries/china clay mining
ECC International Ltd **26**

Miniature cottages
John Hine Ltd **34**

Musical instruments
Boosey & Hawkes Musical Instruments Ltd **44**

P

Pencil-making
Cumberland Pencil Museum & Exhibition Centre **26**

Pottery/ceramics/porcelain/china
Belleek Pottery Ltd **88**
CH Brannam Ltd **29**
Boscastle Pottery **23**
Chessell Pottery (IOW) Ltd **35**
Culloden Pottery **66**
Denby Pottery Visitor Ctr **28**
Etruria Industrial Museum **50**
Highland China Ltd **66**
Hornsea Pottery **57**
Royal Doulton **50**
Royal Grafton China **51**
Royal Worcester Ltd **35**
Spode **51**
Wedgwood Visitor Centre **51**

Power
Berkeley Power Stn (Nuclear Electric) **32**
Bradwell Power Stn (Nuclear Electric) **32**
British Nuclear Fuels plc **27**
Dounreay **65**
Dungeness Power Stn (Nuclear Electric) **39**
Dinorwig Pumped Storage Power Station **81**
Ffestiniog Pumped Storage Power Station **79**
Hartlepool Power Stn (Nuclear Electric) **22**
Heysham Power Stn (Nuclear Electric) **40**
Hinkley Point Power Stn (Nuclear Electric) **46**
Oldbury Nuclear Power Station (Nuclear Electric) **20, 11**
Pembroke Power Station **78**
Powergen **56**
Scottish Power (Cruachan Power Station) **64**
Sizewell Information Ctr Power Stn (Nuclear Electric) **53**
Trawsfynydd Power Stn (Nuclear Electric) **80**
Wylfa Power Stn (Nuclear Electric) **80**

Printing
Porridge Press Ltd **69**

Continued on next page

Subject index continued

R

Railways
Carnforth Railway Restoration & Engineering Services **40**

Rocking horse manufacturers
Stevenson Brothers Rocking Horse Gallery & Workshop **38**

Rock-making (confectionery)
Coronation Rock Co Ltd **39**

S

Satellite station
Goonhilly Satellite Earth Stn **23**

Scythe works
Abbeydale Industrial Hamlet **57**

Sheepskins
John Wood & Sons (Exmoor) **47**

Shire horses
Bass Museum, Visitor Centre and Shire Horse Stables **47**
Shire Trust & Carriage Museum **26**

Silk mills/silk weaving
Highland Tryst Museum **70**
The Working Silk Museum **31**
Whitchurch Silk Mill **35**

Silversmithing
Harts Silversmiths **33**

Slate mines
Gloddfa Ganol Slate Mine **79**
Inigo Jones & Co Limited **80**
Llechwedd Slate Caverns **79**

Soap making
Port Sunlight Heritage Ctr **44**

Steam model making
Maxwell Hemmens Models **58**

T

Tartan Weaving
Highland Tryst Museum **70**

Telecommunications
Telecom Technology Showcase **42**

Tennis
Wimbledon Tennis Museum **43**

Textiles & textile design
James Johnston & Co of Elgin **68**
Thursley Textile Designs **54**
The Cambrian Factory **81**

Textile printers
David Evans & Company **38**

Tin Mines
Geevor Tin Mines & Museum **23**

Tool-making
Finch Foundry and Museum **30**

Tractor manufacturers
Massey-Ferguson Tractors Ltd **55**

Transport systems
Eurotunnel Exhibition Ctr **38**

Tweeds
The Cambrian Factory **81**

U

Underwater discovery
Deep Sea Adventure **30**

W

Watermills
J. Ellis & Sons (Bordon) Ltd **34**
Finch Foundry & Museum of Waterpower **30**
Lower City Mills **70**
John Ridley Projects Ltd **69**

Whisky distilleries
Allied Distillers Ltd **71**
Bunnahabhain Distillery **64**
Glenturret Distillery Ltd **69**
William Grant & Sons Ltd **65**
The 'Old Bushmills' Distillery Company Ltd **88**
John Walker & Son **65**
Scotch Whisky Heritage Ctr **68**

Wine/vineyards
Harveys Wine Museum **20**
Highland Wineries **66**
Lamberhurst Vineyards **39**
Meon Valley Vineyards **34**
North Wootton Vineyard **47**
Priory Vineyards **31**
Thames Valley Vineyard **21**

Wool/weaving
The Cambrian Factory **81**
Coldharbour Mill **29**
Highland Tryst Museum **70**
James Johnston & Co **68**

POWERGEN

PowerGen welcomes parties of visitors to power stations.

Arrangements should be made by writing to the Administrative Officer at the station of your choice.

Location of power stations

Castle Donington (Coal) Phone: 0332 810422	Elland (Coal) Phone: 0422 73341	Grain (Oil) Phone: 0634 271681	Kingsnorth (Coal/Oil) Phone: 0634 250088
Carrington (Coal) Phone: 061 775 3993	Ferrybridge 'B' (Coal) Phone: 0977 672611	Hams Hall (Coal) Phone: 0675 462071	Ratcliffe-on-Soar Phone: 0602 830642/9
Cottam (Coal) Phone: 077784 331	Ferrybridge 'C' (Coal) Phone: 0977 674188	High Marnham (Coal) Phone: 077785 333	Rheidol Hydro Scheme (Hydro) Phone: 097084 667
Drakelow 'B' & 'C' (Coal) Phone: 0283 63341	Fiddler's Ferry (Coal) Phone: 051 424 2020	Ince (Oil) Phone: 09282 3511	Richborough (Oil/Wind) Phone: 0304 612909

PowerGen plc

Wedgwood
Welcomes Visitors

Award-winning museum and art galleries
Cinema video on 230 years of history and craftsmanship
Highly skilled potters and decorators producing tableware and giftware
Extensive souvenir shop
Refreshments lounge
Ample free parking for cars and coaches

VISITOR CENTRE OPENING TIMES
Mon-Fri 9.00am-5.00pm (inc. Bank Holidays)
Saturdays 10.00am-4.00pm. Summer Sundays 10.00am-4.00pm (Easter to October)
Closed Christmas week and New Year's Day

OPEN SUNDAYS EASTER TO OCTOBER

Barlaston, Stoke-on-Trent ST12 9ES
Telephone: (0782) 204141 & (0782) 204218 (24 hrs)

Facilities for disabled people

This symbol is used throughout this guide to show those establishments suitable for disabled people. The establishments listed here have confirmed that they can comply with the following access requirements.

1. At least one entrance must have no steps or be equipped with a ramp whose gradient does not exceed 1:12. The entrance door must have a clear opening width of at least 80cm.

2. A lift giving access to visitor areas must have clear gate opening of at least 80cm; the lift must be at least 140cm deep and 110cm wide.

3. Doors giving access to any of the visitor areas (including WC facilities) must have at least 75cm clear opening width.

Abbeydale Industrial Hamlet **57**
Belleek Pottery Limited **88**
Boscastle Pottery **23**
British Nuclear Fuels plc **27**
Cadbury World **55**
Caithness Glass plc **70**
The Cambrian Factory **81**
Carnforth Railway Restoration & Engineering Services **40**
C H Brannam Limited **29**
Cheddleton Flint Mill **50**
Chessell Pottery (IOW) Limited **35**
Colonial Candle Company Limited **27**
Culloden Pottery **66**
Coloroll Edinburgh Crystal **67**
The Cumberland Pencil Museum & Exhibition Centre **26**
Dartington Crystal **29**
David Evans & Company **38**
Dean Heritage Centre **32**
Deep Sea Adventure **30**
Dinorwig Pump Storage Power Station **81**
Easton Farm Park **53**
Eurotunnel Exhibition Centre **38**
Fleet Air Arm Museum **47**
Gloddfa Ganol Slate Mine **79**
Goonhilly Satellite Earth Station **23**
Hartlepool Nuclear Power Station **22**
Hebridean Jewellery **71**
Heredities Limited **26**
Highland China Limited **66**
Hornsea Pottery **57**
House of Hardy Limited **45**
Inigo Jones & Company Ltd **80**
James Johnston & Co of Elgin Limited **68**
John Taylor Bellfoundry & Museum **41**
John Wood & Sons (Exmoor) Limited **47**
Lathkill Dale Craft Centre **27**
Llechwedd Slate Caverns **79**
London Docklands Development Corp **42**
Longdown Dairy Farm **34**
Lower City Mills **70**
Maude Walkely Clogs **57**
Meon Valley Vineyard **34**
Newmarket Equine Tours **53**
Norfolk Rural Life Museum **45**
Nuclear Electric (Bradwell) **32**
Nuclear Electric (Heysham) **40**
Nuclear Electric (Hinkley Point) **46**
Nuclear Electric (Trawsfynydd) **80**
Oldbury Nuclear Power Station **20**
Pembroke Power Station **78**
Priory Vineyards **31**
Quarry Bank Mill **22**
Redesdale Dairy **46**
Royal Worcester Limited **35**
Sacrewell Farm and Country Centre **21**
Scotch Whisky Heritage Centre **68**
Scotherbs **69**
Shire Horse Trust & Carriage Museum **26**
Sizewell Information Centre **53**
South Leaze Sheep Farm **56**
Stockwood Craft Museum **20**
Summerlee Heritage Trust **67**
Tattenhall Dairy Products Limited **21**
Thames Barrier Visitor Centre **43**
The Thames Valley Vineyard **21**
Thursley Textile Design **54**
Tilbec **33**
Tower Bridge **43**
Tutbury Crystal Glass Limited **50**
Tyrone Crystal **88**
Walsall Leather Centre Museum **56**
Wedgwood Visitor Centre **51**
William Grant & Sons Limited **65**
The Wimbledon Lawn Tennis Museum **43**
The Working Silk Museum **31**
Yorkshire Mining Museum **58**

England

In town or country, people can be found at work all over England on a huge range of activities. Time-honoured crafts such as potting and textile weaving co-exist happily alongside the very latest in hi-tech industry. Whether it's in agriculture or aviation, at a brewery or a brickworks, and there's a whole alphabet of fascinating things for you to see.

Look through the listings in these pages and see what interests you most. Some of them cover industries that form the backbone of daily life, others reflect rare and specialised skills that are unique to the people you can see using them.

Wherever you go, you'll come away knowing just that little bit more about how the world around you fits together. So take a closer look at what goes on in England, and see for yourself just what makes that special 'English difference'. There's a good deal more than meets the eye . . .

England – spoiled for choice!

Two hundred years ago and more, England was the birthplace of the Industrial Revolution, and the story of the great triumphs of those bygone days rightly has its place in our heritage. But no industry survives by dwelling entirely in its past, and many of the visitor centres in these pages have their roots very firmly in the present.

HI-TECH AND LOW TECH!

You can see behind the scenes at such modern technological marvels as the Thames Barrier, or watch the City at work in the futuristic Lloyd's building in the very heart of London. On a more rural tack, you can cast your eye over the fascinating routines of farms of many different kinds, in some of the most delightful parts of the country. If you know where to go — and we can tell you — you can even see racehorses being trained, and perhaps pick up a few useful tips into the bargain! If you like learning how things are put together, then the choice is all yours — you'll find everything from pencils to tractors, from musical instruments to chocolates, each process explained to you in careful detail by people who really do know what they're talking about.

ONE STOP SHOPPING!

Over the years a number of England's leading industries have established themselves as particular favourites with visitors — breweries, potteries, textile factories and so on. As well as the fascination of expertly guided tours you'll often find factory shops selling their goods below shop prices and the irresistible lure of the so-called 'seconds' for the dedicated bargain hunter. But this kind of thing is becoming increasingly common with many much smaller crafts and trades, which is why it pays to take a good look around to see just what's available. Whether it's just for a day out or as one of the highlights of your holiday, you'll never be more spoiled for choice.

AVON

Bristol

Harveys Wine Museum

12 Denmark Street, Bristol, Avon BS1 5DQ
☎ (0272) 277661
Contact: Ms T Spencer, Booking Organiser

13th century cellars of Harveys of Bristol founded in 1796. The home of Bristol Cream sherry now houses fine collections of antique glass, silver, production equipment etc. Tour (2-2½ hrs) of museum displays and video plus tasting of sherries, ports or wines. Shop, also mail order.
Admission: No appointment necessary for tours on Fri only 10.00-12.00 hrs all year (excl Public Holidays). Guided tours Mon-Fri at other times by appointment only. Suitable for individuals and groups of up to 50 (age 18+). From £2.50, Fri £1.50.
Directions: Just off city centre. Nearest railway station: Bristol Temple Meads (1 mile). Nearest bus station: Bristol (½ mile).

R S

Oldbury Nuclear Power Station

Oldbury Waite, Thornbury, Bristol, Avon BS12 1RQ
☎ (0454) 416631
Contact: Ms B Fensome, Visits Organiser

Production of electricity to the national grid utilising nuclear power. Guided tours (1½ hrs) at 10.30, 14.00 and 19.00 hrs. Introductory video on Oldbury Power Station and other video films as appropriate.
Admission: By appointment (24 hrs notice required). Open all year (excl Public Holidays). Last admission 19.00 hrs. Suitable for individuals, school parties (age 9+) and groups of up to 40 people. Free. Brochure and leaflets available.

Please mention this guide when making a booking.

Directions: M5 junct 14 and then by A38 southbound. Turn right to Thornbury and follow signs for Oldbury-on-Severn. Nearest railway station: Bristol Parkway (12 miles). Nearest bus station: Thornbury (5 miles).
See advertisement page 11

CP D V

BEDFORDSHIRE

Luton

Stockwood Craft Museum

Stockwood Park, Luton, Bedfordshire LU1 4BH
☎ (0582) 36941
Contact: Mr F Hackett, Curator

Luton Museum and Art Gallery Wardown Park, Luton LU2 7HX Group of craft workshops which are leased to craftsmen. Situated in 'Craft Courtyard' attached to the museum. Visitors can see traditional crafts including pottery, woodturning, leatherwork, needlework etc. Craftsmen can be seen at work.
Admission: No appointment necessary. Open Mar-Oct Wed-Sat 10.00-17.00 hrs, Sun 10.00-18.00 hrs. Suitable for individuals, families, school parties (ages 5-16) and groups of up to 30 people. Free. Products for sale and commissions accepted.
Directions: From M1 junct 10 follow signs. Nearest railway and bus station: Luton (2 miles).

(40) CP D S

BERKSHIRE

Lambourn

Lambourn Trainers Association

c/o Seven Barrows, Lambourn, Berkshire RG16 7UJ
☎ (0488) 71700
Contact: Mr M Francis, Folly House, Upper Lambourn, Berkshire RG16 7OG
☎ (0488) 71700

The training of racehorses. Visitors will see horses in their stables and on exercise. Guided tours (2 hrs) at 10.00 hrs.
Admission: By appointment only (min notice 4 weeks). Open Sat 10.00-12.00 hrs

(excl Bank Holidays). Suitable for individuals, families, school parties and groups of up to 40 people. Adults and OAPs £5 (+ VAT). Possible shares in horses can be bought. Orders by arrangement.
Directions: M4 junct 14 and follow signs to Lambourn. Nearest railway station: Newbury (15 miles).

CP V

Reading

The Thames Valley Vineyard

Stanlake Park, Twyford, Reading,
Berkshire RG10 0BN
☎ (0734) 340176 or 320025
Contact: Ms White, Director (Functions)

Winery in an historic 17th century barn producing high quality wines from own vineyard planted in 1979. Depending on the season, vines are pruned, trimmed and harvested and wines pressed, filtered and bottled. Guided tours (1½-2 hrs). Winery viewing area and cellar door wine sales.
Admission: Adults only in groups of 10-50 by appointment (min notice 10 days). Winery open all year. £3-10 per person depending on group size
Directions: Turn off A4 to Twyford, take B3018 (signposted Bracknell). Entrance on left shortly after roundabout (Waltham Chase and Stanlake Lane). Nearest railway station: Twyford (½ mile). Nearest coach station: Twyford (¾ mile).

(30+) CP D V S

CAMBRIDGESHIRE

Peterborough

Sacrewell Farm and Country Centre

Sacrewell, Thornhaugh, Peterborough,
Cambridgeshire PE8 6HJ
☎ (0780) 782222
Contact: Mr D Powell, Manager

Large modern farm with historical background. Water mill dates from Domesday. Traditional tools and techniques. Small livestock section. Conservation in the context of a modern farm. Farming according to season, the working water mill and bygones collection. Guided tours (1½ hrs) by appointment. Demonstrations of working water mill.
Admission: Appointment required for groups (min notice 1 week). Open daily 11.00-17.30 hrs. Suitable for individuals, families, school parties (ages 5-18) and groups of 15+ people. Adults £2, OAPs and children £1.50. Shop open 11.00-17.30 hrs. Fruit for sale already picked or pick your own in season.
Directions: Access off A47, 8 miles west of Peterborough. Nearest railway and bus stations: Stamford (5 miles) and Peterborough (8 miles).

(80) CP D V SB S

CHESHIRE

Chester

Tattenhall Dairy Products Limited

Drumlan Hall, Newton Lane, Tattenhall,
Nr Chester, Cheshire CH3 9NE
☎ (0929) 70995
Contact: Mr T L Fell, Director

Working dairy farm which for the past 3 years has manufactured and supplied real dairy ice cream using milk produced from its own dairy herd. Visitors can watch cows being milked (please telephone for times). For pre-booked parties there is a short talk with visual displays showing the ice cream-making process. Unguided tours (1-1½ hrs).
Admission: No appointment neccessary for individuals and families. Advance notice needed for coach parties (max seating capacity for visitors 120). Open all year every day (excl Christmas/New Year) 10.30-17.30 hrs (1 Apr-31 Oct), 11.00-17.00 hrs (1 Nov-31 Mar). Last admission 16.00 hrs for coach parties booked for cream teas. Free. Shop.
Directions: From Chester travel south on A41 Chester-Whitchurch road. Follow Tourist Board signs for 'Ice Cream Farm'. Nearest railway station and coach station: Chester (10 miles).

CP D SB S

ENGLAND

ENGLAND

Stockport

Frederic Robinson Limited

Unicorn Brewery, Stockport, Cheshire
SK1 1JJ
☎ 061-480 6571
Contact: Mrs L Allenby-Carr, Visitor Guide & Organiser

The brewery is run by an independent company which has been brewing since 1838. Guided tours (2 hrs), video presentation about Company. Products for sale. **Admission:** Tours available all year by appointment only (min notice 12 months). Suitable for groups of 15-25 people. Free. **Directions:** From M63 take Stockport East (exit). Nearest railway and bus stations: Stockport (½ mile).

🚗 CP V S

Wilmslow

Quarry Bank Mill

Styal, Nr Wilmslow, Cheshire SK9 4LA
☎ (0625) 527468
Contact: Ms A Ferguson, Publicity Officer

Georgian cotton mill now an award-winning museum with large working waterwheel set in millworkers' village. Produces cloth on traditional looms. Hand spinning and weaving demonstrations, machine spinning mule. Tours of mill and apprentice house. Visual presentations. Shop. Orders taken for textiles. **Admission:** No appointment necessary. Open daily Apr-Sept 11.00-17.00 hrs, Oct-Mar (excl Mon) 11.00-16.00 hrs. Suitable for individuals, families, school parties (age 6+) and groups. Adults £3.75 (mill only £2.75), OAPs and children £2.75 (mill only £2). Reductions for groups of 20+ people. **Directions:** 10 miles south of Manchester, 2 miles from Manchester Airport. From M56 junct 5, fully signposted. Nearest railway station: Wilmslow (1½ miles). Nearest bus station: Manchester (10 miles).
See advertisement page **59**

🚗 (300) CP D V R SB S

CLEVELAND

Hartlepool

Hartlepool Nuclear Power Station

Energy Information Centre, Tees Road, Hartlepool, Cleveland TS25 2BZ
☎ (0429) 869201/2. Contact: Mrs L Eccles

Nuclear power station for generation of electricity. 'Generations of Energy' an exciting audio visual show, which tells the history of energy and electricity generation including nuclear energy. Guided tours of power station by arrangement (1¼ hrs), video (1 hr). **Admission:** By appointment (min notice 1 week). Energy Information Centre open all year (excl Public Holidays) Mon-Fri 09.00-16.00 hrs. Last admission 15.00 hrs. Evening and weekend opening by arrangement. Suitable for individuals, school parties and groups of up to 100 people. Free. **Directions:** Take A19 to A689 and then follow road to first roundabout and take second exit to Seal Sands (A1185). Turn left at next roundabout on to A178. Follow road to next roundabout, turn right. Nearest railway and bus station: Hartlepool (4 miles).
See advertisement page 11.

🚗 (100) CP D V

Whitbread & Company plc

PO Box 13, Castle Eden, Hartlepool, Cleveland TS27 4SX. ☎ (0429) 836431
Contact: Mr J L S Ogden, Head Brewer & General Manager

The brewery was founded in 1826 and purchased by Whitbread's in 1964. Traditional beers are brewed including Castle Eden and Best Scotch. Depending on time of visit and production levels, beer brewing, processing and racking can be seen by visitors. Guided tours (1½ hrs). Video film 'The Brewers Craft'. **Admission:** By appointment (21 days notice required). Open Jan-Nov Mon-Thur 10.00-15.00 hrs (excl Public Holidays). Last admission 15.00 hrs. Suitable for school parties (age 16+) and groups of 10-30 people. Adults £3.50, Children £3, OAPs £2.50. Products sold during visit. **Directions:** Situated in Castle Eden at the junct of A19 and A181.

🚗 (10) CP V S

CORNWALL

Boscastle

Boscastle Pottery

The Old Bakery, Boscastle, Cornwall
PL35 0HE
☎ (084 05) 291
Contact: Mr R Irving-Little, Potter

Long-established family pottery specialising in Mochaware, a form of pottery decorated with a herb which creates a tree and fern effect. Demonstrations of throwing and decorating and a chance to talk to the potters. Shop. Display of crystals and fossils.
Admission: No appointment necessary. Open all year every day 09.00 hrs-dusk. Suitable for individuals, groups and school parties of up to 25 people. Free.
Directions: On the B3263 200 yds from harbour. Nearest railway station: Bodmin Parkway (15 miles).

CP D S

Helston

Goonhilly Satellite Earth Station

Goonhilly Downs, Helston, Cornwall
TR12 6LQ
☎ (0872) 45400; visitors (0872) 45325
Contact: Mr J Macknelly, Publicity Manager

Goonhilly is a working satellite earth station comprising of 7 large dish aerials. Provides communications with the rest of the world for British Telecom. Guided tour (1 hr) of the operations control centre with close look at aerials incl explanation of how an international phone call is made from Edinburgh to USA.
Admission: No appointment necessary from Easter-Oct 10.00-18.00 hrs. By appointment only Oct-Easter min notice of 48 hrs required. Last admission 18.00 hrs. Suitable for individuals, families, school parties and groups. Adults £2.50, OAPs and children (age 5+) £1.50. Reduced rates for groups of 20+ people.
Directions: From A30 at Redruth, follow signs to Helston. From Helston take A3083 to the Lizard. Turn left past Naval Air Station on to B3293 (St Keverne Road) and follow signs. Nearest railway station: Redruth (20 miles).

(400) CP D V R

Penhallow

Callestock Cider Farm

Penhallow, Truro, Cornwall TR4 9LW
☎ (0872) 573356
Contact: Mr D Healey, Managing Director

A family-run farm producing scrumpy cider, country wines, jams and preserves. Friendly farm animals, orchards, tractor rides and museum of cider and farming antiquities. From growing the fruit to bottling can be seen subject to season. Video. Guided tours (1 hr) by appointment (min 20 people).
Admission: No appointment necessary (except for guided tours). Open Easter-Dec Mon-Fri 09.00-17.00 hrs plus May-Oct Sat 09.00-18.00 hrs. In Jul and Aug late opening till 20.00 hrs. Suitable for individuals, school parties and groups. Free to overall attraction but adults £1.50, OAPs & children 75p for museum & tractor rides. Products for sale.
Directions: Signposted from Penhallow on the A3075 Newquay to Redruth road. Nearest railway and bus station: Truro (5 miles).

(100) CP S

Penzance

Geevor Tin Mines and Museum

Pendeen, Penzance, Cornwall TR19 7EW
☎ (0736) 788662
Contact: Ms D Paynter, Tourist Amenity Mgress

Tin mine under the sea. Underground tours 2,100 ft down and ¼ mile out under sea. Tour mineral processing plant, mining museum, the walk—old Levant mine including beam engine. Visitors see mining for tin underground and, on the surface, ore processing, tin extraction, mining museum, video show. Guided tours: underground (2½ hrs), surface (1½ hrs) 10.30-16.00 hrs. Products for sale.
Admission: No appointment necessary. Open Easter-Oct (incl Bank Holidays) Sun-Fri 10.00-17.30 hrs. Suitable for individuals, families, school parties (ages 7-16) and groups of 10-60 people. Adults £12.50 (or £2.75 surface only), OAPs £12.50 (or £2.25 surface only), children (age 14+) £1.50 (surface only). Reduced group rates £11 (or £2.25 surface only).
Directions: A30 to Penzance, A3071 to St Just then B3318 to Pendeen. Nearest railway and bus station: Penzance (7 miles).

(200) CP V SB S

ENGLAND

What's brewing?

Traditional British beer is brewed from the simplest and best of ingredients — just malted barley, water and hops. The malted (ie germinated) barley is first ground into grist and then hot water — known as 'liquor' in brewing terminology — is added to form a mash. Many brewers maintain that the quality of the local water gives their beer its distinctive character.

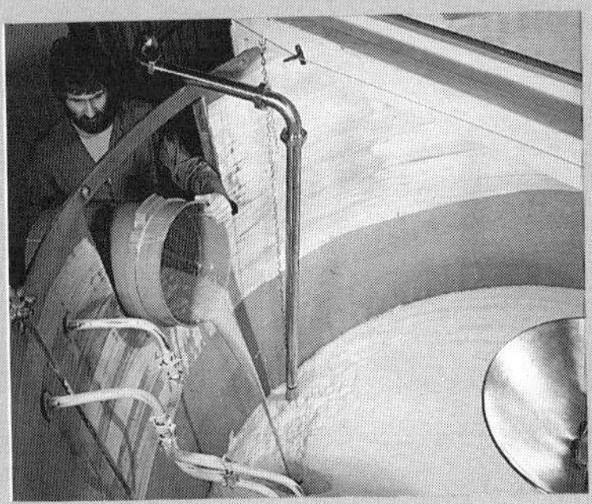

THE TASTE OF HOPS

Natural sugars are dissolved out of the grist before the liquid or 'wort' is run off into a huge copper. Here the wort is boiled with hops, which give the beer its bitter taste. Our distant ancestors preferred ale, which in simple terms is unhopped beer — it has a much sweeter taste. Ale goes off very quickly but the hops used in beer-making act as a natural preservative and help kill off bacteria. When the wort is ready for the yeast to be added in, the fermentation process can begin. With beer, the yeast is tipped into the copper, but lager is made by 'bottom fermentation', in which the yeast is introduced into the wort from below. Yeast is a living organism, and many breweries have maintained their own special strain over the years to ensure continuity. During fermentation — which typically takes around five days, but is often longer — the sugars in the wort turn into alcohol.

THE MATURATION PROCESS

If the beer is to be served in the traditional way — via a handpump or even direct from the barrel — it will now be matured for several days in a conditioning tank before being racked into barrels. Further hops and a quantity of sugar may be added at this stage so that the beer will continue to ferment in the barrel. Alternatively, this secondary fermentation may take place in a tank. Because traditionally conditioned beer is alive, its flavour and character are allowed to develop subtly right up until the moment it is served in the pub.

BEER UNDER PRESSURE

It is, however, difficult to keep cask-conditioned beer at its best without a great deal of skilled attention from the landlord. Instead some breweries prefer to produce pasteurised beers — lager for instance, as well as so-called keg bitter — which are stored and dispensed under carbon dioxide pressure to improve their stability. Canned or bottled beers and lagers are made in the same way. Such brewery-conditioned beer is filtered to remove all traces of yeast and thus prevent secondary fermentation. These beers keep well and are easy to store and serve — usually chilled — but they can never quite match the flavour and aroma of a beer that has been allowed to mature the natural way. Britain is the only country in the world where traditionally brewed beers are still served in the time-honoured manner, and this goes a long way towards creating the character of that great national institution, the English pub.

Redruth

Shire Horse Trust & Carriage Museum

Lower Gryllis, Treskillard, Redruth, Cornwall TR16 6LA
☎ (0209) 713606
Contact: Mr H J Gotts, Owner

Lady blacksmith, wheelwrights and farrier working at Museum. Visitors can see general blacksmithing work, shoeing horses and making wheels. Guided tours (2 hrs) available 10.00-16.00 hrs. Demonstrations given of work in progress. Products for sale, orders accepted.
Admission: No appointment necessary. Open daily Easter-Oct 10.00-16.00 hrs. Suitable for individuals, families, school parties and groups. Max capacity 500 people. Adults and OAPs £2.25, children £1.25.
Directions: Leave Camborne By-Pass at Pool turn off. Across traffic lights past Homeworld and turn right over railway bridge. Turn left, then right and carry on to Treskillard sign. Nearest railway stations: Redruth or Camborne (1½ miles). Nearest bus station: Camborne (1½ miles).

(300) CP D SB S

St Austell

ECC International Limited

John Keay House, St Austell, Cornwall PL25 4DJ
☎ (0726) 74482
Contact: Mrs S Over, Public Relations Assistant

ECC produces industrial minerals worldwide. On view at Gunmeath China Clay Quarry are large scale opencast mining operations and processing plants for some of the 2.5 million tonnes of china clay produced in Cornwall for the paper, ceramics and plastics industries. Tours (1½ hrs) at 10.00-14.00 hrs.
Admission: By appointment (min notice 2 weeks). Open all year (excl Public Holidays and Factory Holidays) Mon-Fri 10.00-11.30 hrs and 14.00-15.30 hrs. Suitable for individuals, families, school parties and groups of up to 40 people. Free.
Directions: Off A391 St Austell to Bugle Rd nr Carthew. Maps are sent to visitors. Nearest railway and bus stations: St Austell (2½ miles).

(10) CP

CUMBRIA

Keswick

The Cumberland Pencil Museum and Exhibition Centre

Southey Works, Keswick, Cumbria CA12 5NG
☎ (076 87) 73626
Contact: Ms S Corfield, Museum Supervisor

The museum traces the history of pencil-making from the discovery of Borrowdale graphite in the 1500s through early cottage industry to modern production methods. Tours (approx 1 hr) covering pencil manufacture and the use of Derwent Watercolour Pencils.
Admission: No appointment necessary. Open all year (excl Christmas/New Year) 09.30-16.00 hrs. Last admission time 16.00 hrs. Suitable for individuals, families and school parties (up to age 16) and groups of 10-25 people. Adults £1, OAPs and children 50p. Pre-booked groups: adults 75p, OAPs/children 35p. Visitors can purchase goods from shop.
Directions: From M6 junct 40, take A66 to Keswick to west of town and Museum is 300 yds past bus station. Nearest railway station: Penrith (19 miles). Nearest bus/coach stations: Keswick (300 yds).

(50) D S

Kirkby Stephen

Heredities Limited

Kirkby Stephen, Cumbria CA17 4QY
☎ (076 83) 71543
Contact: Ms A Smith, PR Officer

Manufacturers of figurines in cold cast bronze and hand painted resin. Photographs showing procedures available.
Admission: No appointment necessary. Open Mon-Fri 09.00-17.00 hrs. Last admission 16.45 hrs. Suitable for individuals and families. Max capacity 15 visitors. Free. Products for sale including seconds, firsts, discontinued lines.
Directions: M6 junct 38 Tebay to Kirkby Stephen. Leave town, turn left at advance factory sign, then first right into Hobsons Lane. Nearest railway station: Kirkby (½ mile).

(15-20) D S

Seascale

British Nuclear Fuels plc

Sellafield Visitors Centre, Seascale, Cumbria CA20 1PG
☎ (094 67) 27027
Contact: Mr C L Tuley, Public Relations Officer

Britain's first industrial scale nuclear power station and spent nuclear fuel reprocessing plant. Displays in visitor centre explain nuclear power process. Guided tours and plant visits to see various aspects of reprocessing in progress. Wide variety of presentations. Shop.
Admission: No appointment necessary for visitor centre. Notice required for plant tours. Open all year (excl 25 Dec). Apr-Oct 10.00-18.00 hrs, Nov-Dec 10.00-16.00 hrs. Suitable for individuals, families, groups and school parties. Free.
Directions: From M6 junct 40, take A66 towards Workington, then A595 south. Nearest railway station: Sellafield (2 miles). Nearest bus station: Whitehaven (11 miles). See advertisement page 16.

🚗 (120+) CP D V R S

Ulverston

Colonial Candle Company Limited

Lindal Business Park, Lindal-in-Furness, Ulverston, Cumbria LA12 0LL
☎ (0229) 66272. Fax (0229) 66769
Contact: Ms L Shepherd, Director

Manufacturers of an impressive range of candles in many styles, colours and fragrances which together with colour co-ordinating kitchen textiles and ceramics, are sold at factory prices in shop. Visitors can see hand moulding and hand dipping of candles. Guided tours (20-30 mins) if required.
Admission: No appointment necessary for individuals and small groups of up to 20 people. 24 hrs for larger groups. Open all year Mon-Sat 09.00-17.00 hrs. Suitable for individuals, families, school parties (age 10+) and groups of 20-50 people. Max capacity 50 people. Free. Products can be bought in shop.
Directions: From M6 junct 36, take A590 to Barrow for approx 20 miles Lindal-in-Furness. Turn left and factory is 100 yds away. Nearest railway/bus stations: Ulverston (3 miles).

🚗 (40) CP D S

Stott Park Bobbin Mill

Finsthwaite, Nr Ulverton, Cumbria LA12 8AX
☎ (053 95) 31087
Contact: Mr T Martin, Asst Marketing Mgr, English Heritage, 429 Oxford Street, London W1R 2HD ☎ 071-973 3421

A unique opportunity to hear and see how the little known bobbin making industry began and in the modern age of plastic perhaps inevitably declined. Much of the machinery still remains, this includes a turbine and steam engine. Guided tours (45 mins).
Admission: No appointment necessary. Open daily 1 Apr-31 Oct 10.00-18.00 hrs. Closes at dusk if earlier. Suitable for individuals, families, school parties and groups of 11-20 people. Adults £1.40, OAPs £1.05, children 70p. Special reduced rates for groups (15% discount for groups of 11+). Children must be accompanied by an adult.
Directions: ½ mile north of Finsthwaite nr Newby Bridge on road from Lakeside-Hawkshead.

🚗 (50) CP

DERBYSHIRE

Bakewell

Lathkill Dale Craft Centre

Over Haddon, Bakewell, Derbyshire DE4 1JE
☎ (0629) 813589
Contact: Mrs C Pearce, Partner

Ceramics, stained glass, wood-turning, furniture making, antique clock and barometer repairs, jewellery and silversmithing and the making of children's clothes demonstrated by crafts people in workshops in beautifully converted old stone farm buildings situated around an attractive courtyard.
Admission: No appointment necessary. Suitable for individuals, families, school parties and groups. Open all year (excl Christmas Day & Boxing Day) 10.00-17.00 hrs. Free. Gift shop. Crafts people take orders/commissions.
Directions: M1 southbound to junct 30 then A616 Chesterfield (or junct 29 then A617 Chesterfield) and A619 to Bakewell, then B5055 turning off to Over Haddon. Nearest railway station: Buxton or Matlock (11 miles). Nearest coach station: Bakewell (2 miles).

🚗 (50) CP D SB S

ENGLAND

Denby

Denby Pottery Visitor Centre

Denby Pottery, Denby, Nr Derby, Derbyshire DE5 8NX
☎ (0773) 743641
Contact: Mr P Lowe, Manager, Visitor Centre

Manufacturers of high quality stoneware (tableware, giftware and cookware) products. Visitors can see throwing, turning, jolleying, casting, handling and glazing. Guided tours (50 mins).
Admission: No appointment necessary for individuals but appointment required for groups (min notice 48 hrs). Open all year (excl Public Holidays) Mon-Thur 09.00-15.00 hrs, Fri 09.00-11.30 hrs. Last admission 15.00 hrs for tours and open every day (excl Christmas/New Year) for other facilities. Suitable for individuals, families, school parties (age 8+) and groups of up to 100 people. Adults £1.50, OAPs and children 80p. No photography allowed. Shop.
Directions: On B6179 2 miles south of Ripley, 8 miles north of Derby. Nearest railway station: Alfreton (5 miles). Nearest bus station: Derby (8 miles).

🚗 (100) CP V R SB S

Eckington

Ridgeway Cottage Industry Centre

Kent House Farm, Ridgeway, Nr Eckington, Derbyshire S12 3XR
☎ (0742) 477028
Contact: Senior Estates Officer, North East Derbyshire District Council, Planning Dept, Estate Office, Saltergate, Chesterfield, Derbyshire S40 1LF. ☎ (0246) 231111

Ridgeway Cottage Industry Centre, converted from a 300-year-old derelict farm is situated in the attractive village of Ridgeway. Opened May 1987. 14 craft workshops including blacksmith, stained glass maker, chocolatier, candle maker, leatherworker etc. Demonstrations.
Admission: No appointment necessary. Open all year Tue-Sun 10.30-17.00 hrs. Closed Mon (excl Bank Holidays). Suitable for individuals, groups and school parties. No access for disabled to first floor. Products for sale in shop 10.30-17.00 hrs. Orders accepted for some crafts.
Directions: M1 junct 30, then A616 to Eckington through Mosborough to B6054, signposted Ridgeway. Nearest railway and bus station: Chesterfield (8 miles).

🚗 V R SB S

DEVON

Barnstaple

C H Brannam Limited

Roundswell Industrial Estate, Barnstaple,
Devon EX31 3NJ
☎ (0271) 43035
Contact: Mr S D Fox, Managing Director

Established over 100 years the Company moved to new site in 1989. Manufacturer of terracotta ware and Mr Brannam cookware. Suppliers of porcelain and oriental planters. Visitors can see potters at the wheel and decorators plus the processes of manufacture. Guided tours (¾ hr). Demonstrations of hand throwing and hand decorating available most of the day.
Admission: No appointment necessary. Open all year. Tours Mon-Sat 09.00-17.00 hrs plus Sun (July-Aug) 10.00-16.00 hrs. Suitable for individuals, school parties (age 5+) and groups of 4-25 people. Adults £1.50, OAPs £1.25, children (ages 5-16) 75p. Shop.
Directions: On southern side of Barnstaple signposted from new A39 road to Bideford. Nearest railway station: Barnstaple (1 mile). Nearest bus station: The Strand (1¼ miles).

🚗 (200) CP D R S

Budleigh Salterton

Otterton Mill Limited

Fore Street, Otterton, Budleigh Salterton,
Devon EX9 7HG
☎ (0395) 68521/68031
Contact: Mrs D Greenhow, Director

Water-powered flour mill producing stone-ground wholemeal and unbleached white and rye flours. Visitors can see mill museum, milling with part-wooden machinery, using breastshot waterwheel. Tours (½ hr). Shop.
Admission: No appointment necessary. Open Easter to end-Oct daily 10.30-17.30 hrs, rest of year 11.30-16.30 hrs. Suitable for individuals, families, school parties (ages (5-18) and groups of 12-100 people. Adults £1.25, children 70p. Group reductions.
Directions: Off A376, 2 miles from Budleigh Salterton. Nearest railway station: Exmouth (6 miles). Nearest bus station: Exeter (15 miles).

🚗 (30) CP R S

Cullompton

Coldharbour Mill

Uffculme, Cullompton, Devon EX15 3EE
☎ (0884) 40960
Contact: Ms J Taylor, Director

A working wool museum producing pure wool knitting yarn. This historic factory has been in production since 1797 and won an award for excellence in heritage education. Old worsted spinning machinery on view. Also carding, mule spinning and weaving. Conducted tours (1 hr). Audio/slide presentation. Shop. Garments knitted to order.
Admission: No appointment necesary. Open Easter-Oct daily 11.00-17.00 hrs. Winter Mon-Fri 11.00-17.00 hrs (visitors are advised to confirm by phone). Suitable for individuals, school parties and groups of 20-90 people. Adults £2.25, children £1.50, groups £2.
Directions: 2 miles from junct 27 on M5, off B3181. Follow signs to Willand and then to museum. Nearest railway station: Tiverton Parkway (2 miles). Nearest bus station: Tiverton (7 miles).

🚗 (80) CP V R S

Great Torrington

Dartington Crystal

Linden Close, School Lane, Great Torrington,
Devon EX38 7AN
☎ (0805) 22321
Contact: Mr S Ackland, Tourism Manager

One of Britain's leading manufacturers of hand-made plain crystal glassware and gifts and one of Devon's top tourist attractions. Factory tours (45-60 mins) Mon-Fri (excl Bank Holidays). Video film and demonstrations.
Admission: No advance appointment necessary for individuals and families, same day notice for groups of 10-60 people. Max capacity 180 people. Open all year Mon-Fri 09.00-17.00 hrs and Sat and Sun 22 July-2 Sept. Closed 21 Dec 1990-7 Jan 1991. Adults £1.40 (75p visitor centre only). Children under 6 free, ages 6-16 yrs 70p (25p visitor centre only). No video cameras or dogs (excl guide dogs). Shop.
Directions: M5 junct 27, then A361 and A39 to Torridge Bridge. Signs from there. Nearest railway station: Barnstaple (11 miles). Nearest coach station: Bideford (7 miles).

🚗 (200) CP D V R S

ENGLAND

ENGLAND

Okehampton

Finch Foundry and Museum of Waterpower

Sticklepath, Okehampton, Devon EX20 2NW
☎ (0837) 840046
Contact: Dr G Irlam, Custodian

Unique 19th century factory on edge of Dartmoor making edge tools like scythes, billhooks and shovels. Now a museum. 3 working waterwheels power massive tilt and drop hammers, shears and grindstone. Guided tours (20 mins +) and demonstrations of machinery available.
Admission: No appointment necessary (except for groups). Open 1 Mar-22 Dec Mon-Sat (plus Sun Apr-Sept) 10.00-17.00 hrs. Last admission 16.30 hrs. Suitable for individuals, families, school parties and groups of 10-50 people. Adults £1.50, OAPs £1.20, children 80p. Reduced rates for groups of 10+ people.
Directions: In centre of Sticklepath village 4 miles east of Okehampton. Signposted from A30 nr Okehampton. Nearest railway and bus stations: Exeter (20 miles).

🚗 (20) CP SB S

South Molton

Quince Honey Farm

North Road, South Molton, Devon
EX36 3AZ
☎ (076 95) 2401
Contact: Mr P Wallace, Partner

Britain's largest honey farm producing quality honey and beeswax products. Exhibition of living honey bees. Depending on season, visitors can see honey extracting and bottling, beeswax candle manufacture and polish making. 5 continuous video shows. Shop selling honeycomb and other products.
Admission: No appointment necessary. Open Easter to end-Sept daily 09.00-18.00 hrs, Oct-Easter 09.00-17.00 hrs. Suitable for individuals, families, school parties (ages 5-18) and groups of 15+ people. Adults £2.45, OAPs £2, children £1.10. Special reduced group rate £1.40.
Directions: From M5 junct 27, take A361. Nearest railway station: Barnstaple (12 miles). Nearest bus station: South Molton (800 yds).

🚗 (200) CP V R S

DORSET

Dorchester

Eldridge Pope & Company plc

Dorchester Brewery, Dorchester, Dorset
DT1 1QT
☎ (0305) 251251
Contact: Ms M Gould

An independent brewer and wine merchant founded in 1837. Guided tours (2 hrs) showing brewery in operation, wine and beer bottling, warehousing and retailing. Presentation on company product histories. Shop.
Admission: By appointment only. Open Mon-Thur. Closed Bank Holidays. Tours at 11.00, 14.30, 19.30 hrs. Suitable for individuals, groups and school parties up to 30 people. Free.
Directions: In Dorchester on A354 Weymouth Road. Nearest railway station: Dorchester South (2 mins).

🚗 (20) CP V S

Weymouth

Deep Sea Adventure

9 Custom House Quay, Old Harbour,
Weymouth, Dorset DT4 8BG
☎ (0305) 760690
Contact: Mr B Cooper, Director

Interpretative display on history of underwater discovery from 17th century to today. 3 floors (9,000 sq ft) of animated displays, sounds, smell and lighting effects. Live diving in high season. Real diving equipment old and modern in operation. Guided tours (1 hr) by appointment only. Shop.
Admission: No appointment necessary except for large groups. Open all year daily (excl Christmas Day, Boxing Day and first 2 weeks Jan) 10.00-17.30 hrs (Jul-Aug 10.00-22.00 hrs). Suitable for individuals, families, school parties (age 5+) and groups of 10-60 people. Adults £2.50, OAPs £2, children £1.50.
Directions: A354 or A35 to Weymouth. Follow signs to Old Harbour. Nearest railway and bus stations: Weymouth (¾ mile).

🚗 (50) CP D V S

ESSEX

Braintree

The Working Silk Museum

New Mills, South Street, Braintree, Essex
Contact: Mr R J Humphries, Partner
Humphries Weaving Company, Devere Mill, Castle Hedingham, Halstead, Essex CO9 3HA
☎ (0787) 61193

The last manufacturers of hand woven silk fabrics on early 19th century looms in England, weaving ceremonial silks and lavish silk furnishings. All processes involved including winding, warping, weaving Jacquard textiles and museum of past work. Guided tours (1 hr) Sat 14.00, 15.00 and 16.00 hrs.
Admission: By appointment for groups (min notice 28 days). Open Easter-Christmas 10.00-17.00 hrs. Closed Sun and Bank Holidays. Evening tours can be arranged for groups only. Last admission 16.00 hrs. Suitable for individuals, school parties (ages 7-12) and groups of 20-55 people. No unaccompanied children under age 16. Products can be bought. Adults £2.25, OAPs and children £1.25.
Directions: M11 & A12 and then on to A120 Braintree by-pass. Nearest railway/bus station: Braintree (¼ mile).

(120) CP D R

Chelmsford

Redman & Hales Limited

The Street, Hatfield Peverel, Chelmsford, Essex CM3 2EQ
☎ (0245) 380322
Contact: Mr S Hales, Managing Director

Specialist makers of solid mahogany period style furniture. All traditional hand work. French polishing. Comprehensive stock. Special commissions undertaken.
Admission: No appointment necessary. Open all year Mon, Tue, Thur, Fri 09.00-12.30 hrs and 13.30-17.00 hrs. Wed 09.00-12.30 hrs. Workshop open Sat 09.00-17.00 hrs but staff not working. Suitable for individuals, families and groups of up to 20 people.
Directions: Hatfield Peverel is signposted on A12 first exit beyond Chelmsford travelling North, or first exit beyond Witham travelling South. Redman & Hales is in main street, Hatfield Peverel. Nearest railway station: Hatfield Peverel (⅔ miles). Nearest bus station: Chelmsford (6 miles).

Little Dunmow

Priory Vineyards

Priory Place, Little Dunmow, Essex CM6 3HY
☎ (0371) 820577
Contact: Col D Cooper, Owner/Partner

10-acre vineyard established in 1981. Main grape varieties are Muller Thurgau, Serval, Ortega, Huxelrebe. Wine can be bought and orders accepted.
Admission: By appointment (min notice 1 day). Open 1 Apr-30 Sept 10.00-16.00 hrs. Suitable for individuals or groups of 10-30 people. Adults £1.50, children 50p.
Directions: On A120 1½ miles east of Dunmow. Turn south towards Little Dunmow. After ⅓ mile turn right into Little Dunmow village, then first right to Grange Lane then first left. 150 yds down track is Priory Vineyard. Nearest railway station: Braintree (5 miles). Buses stop in Little Dunmow (¼ mile).

(20) CP D S

ENGLAND

Southminster

Nuclear Electric

Bradwell Nuclear Power Station,
Bradwell-on-Sea, Southminster, Essex
CM0 7HP
☎ (0621) 76331
Contact: Mr J Miley, Technical Support Officer

Production of electricity by nuclear power. Nuclear reactor, steam turbine, control room and power station plant. Guided tours (2 hrs). Introductory talk and a question and answer session after tour.
Admission: By appointment only (6 weeks notice required). Open all year. Suitable for individuals, families, school parties and groups of 5-40 people. Free.
Directions: A12 Chelmsford by-pass, then A414 via Danbury and Latchingdon to Bradwell. Nearest railway station: Southminster (8 miles).
See advertisement page 11.

(50) CP D V

GLOUCESTERSHIRE

Berkeley

Berkeley Power Station

Nuclear Electric, Berkeley, Gloucestershire
GL13 9PA
☎ (0453) 810431
Contact: Receptionist

Britain's first commercial nuclear power station in operation from 1962-1989, which has twin Magnox reactors and 4-steam turbine generators. Work in progress that can be seen by visitors is the removal of nuclear fuel and preparations and plans for decommissioning. Guided tours (2½ hrs) at 10.00, 14.00 and 19.00 hrs. Presentations showing how electricity is made, nuclear power and the environment.
Admission: By appointment only individuals and small groups (min notice 24 hrs), larger parties of up to 50 people (7 days). Open all year (excl Public Holidays) Mon-Fri (incl evenings), Sat am and pm only. Free.
Directions: M5 junct 13 or 14, A38 and B4066 to Berkeley town centre. Follow sign to Power Station (1½ miles). Nearest railway station: Gloucester or Bristol Parkway (15 miles). Nearest coach station: Berkeley (1½ miles).
See advertisement page 11.

(50) CP V SB

Cinderford

Dean Heritage Centre

Camp Mill, Soudley, Cinderford,
Gloucestershire GL14 7UG
☎ (0594) 22170
Contact: Ms S Ashmole, PR & Education Officer

Museum interpreting natural, industrial and social heritage of Forest of Dean with craft workshops, shop, cafe, smallholding, nature trails, adventure playground and picnic/barbecue sites. Restored beam engine, 12 ft overshot waterwheel plus variety of hand crafts. Guided tour (1 hr). Video.
Admission: No appointment necessary for individuals and families but advance booking preferred for parties. Open all year daily (excl Christmas/Boxing Day). Apr-Oct 10.00-18.00 hrs, Nov-Mar 10.00-17.00 hrs. Suitable for individuals, families, school parties and groups. Adults £2.25, OAPs £1.50, children £1.25. Products for sale, orders accepted.

Directions: On B4227 in village of Soudley between Cinderford and Blakeney. Nearest railway station: Lydney (8 miles). Nearest bus station: Cinderford (3 miles).

(180) CP D R SB S

Chipping Campden

Harts Silversmiths

The Guild, Sheep Street, Chipping Campden, Gloucestershire GL55 6DS
☎ (0386) 841100
Contact: Mr D Hart or Mr D Elliott, Partners

Workshop started in 1902 by architect and designer, C R Ashbee (Guild of Handicraft). Silverwork designed and made by hand to suit customer's requirements. Visitors see the making of large and small articles. Guided tours.
Admission: No appointment necessary for individuals and families. School parties and small groups of up to 7 people by appointment (min notice 2 days). Free. Open all year (excl Public Holidays) Mon-Fri 09.00-17.00 hrs, Sat 09.00-12.00 hrs. Work undertaken and for sale.
Directions: By road to Chipping Campden, workshop on the first floor of an old silk mill in Sheep Street. Nearest railway station and bus/coach stations: Moreton-in-Marsh (9 miles).

S

Tewkesbury

Tilbec

Stables Cottage, Kemerton, Nr Tewkesbury, Gloucestershire GL20 7HY
☎ (038 689) 283
Contact: Ms Tilly M, Owner

Watch Tilly M, the Pied Piemaker of Gloucestershire making hot water crust in her studio kitchen. Be filled to the brim with pure organic old English hand-made pies and puddings. Hear her life story to the accompaniment of live music. Guided tours (3 hrs) incl meal, talk, music.
Admission: By appointment only (min notice 3 days for groups, Sat kitchens 1 day). Open all year daily. Suitable for individuals, families, school parties (age 14+) and groups of 10-53 people. Adults £5.50, £10 or £12.50 (+ VAT) depending on size of meal required. Children £5.50.
Directions: From M5 junct 9 (exit for Tewkesbury), take Evesham Road and then left turn to Bredon Hill and right to Kemerton. Nearest railway station: Evesham (11 miles). Nearest bus station: Cheltenham (12 miles).

(20) CP D

ENGLAND

HAMPSHIRE

Aldershot

John Hine Limited

2 Hillside Road, Aldershot, Hampshire
GU11 3NB
☎ (0252) 334672
Contact: Mr K Mackenzie, Promotions Exec

Creators and manufacturers of David Winter miniature cottages using traditional handcraft techniques. Casting, painting and sculpting demonstrations. Guided tour (1½-2 hrs).
Admission: By appointment (1 week in advance). Open every day (excl Public Holidays and weekends). Tours 10.00, 14.00 hrs. Suitable for individuals, families, school parties and groups of up to 35 people. Free.
Directions: Nearest railway and bus stations: Aldershot (½ mile).

🚗 (20) CP V

Bordon

J Ellis & Sons (Bordon) Limited

Headley Mill, Bordon, Hampshire GU35 8RJ
☎ (042 03) 2031
Contact: Miss S Clinker, Secretary

First recorded AD 978. The earliest manorial traditions of this remarkable family-owned watermill are still being carried on. Water-powered millstones grinding wheat into wholemeal flour and rolling cereals for animals. Guided tours (1-1½ hrs). Demonstration of dressing millstones.
Admission: By appointment only (min notice 48 hrs). Open Apr-Oct Tue-Sat 10.00-17.00 hrs. Last admission 16.00 hrs. Suitable for individuals, families, school parties and groups of 5-60 people. Adults £1, OAPs and accompanied children 50p. No smoking or dogs. Products sold 09.00-17.00 hrs. Orders accepted for stoneground wholemeal.
Directions: 45 miles south of London on tributary of River Wey. On B3004 which connects A3 with A325. Nearest railway station: Liphook (3 miles). Nearest bus station: Hindhead (4 miles).

🚗 (30) CP PS S

Southampton

Longdown Dairy Farm

Longdown, Ashurst, Nr Southampton, Hampshire SO4 4UH
☎ (0703) 293326
Contact: Ms L Holmes, Marketing Assistant
Longdown Estate Office, Longdown, Ashurst, Nr Southampton, Hampshire SO4 4UH

A modern working dairy farm with 150 Friesian cows and a variety of farm animals. Video unit, computerised quiz, picnic area and playground. Visitors can see milking (pm), feeding and general farm management. Guided tours (2-2½ hrs) for groups only.
Admission: No appointment necessary for individuals but appointment required for groups (min notice 1 week). Open daily 7 Apr-28 Oct 11.00-17.00 hrs. Last admission 16.00 hrs. Suitable for individuals, families, school parties and groups of 15+ people. Adults £2.50, OAPs £2.30, children £1.50 (ages 5-16 yrs). Special reduced group rates for adults £2.20 (min 15 people), children £1.30. Gift shop.
Directions: Off A35 between Totton and Ashurst (nr Southampton). Nearest railway station: Lyndhurst Road, Ashurst (2 miles). Nearest bus stop: Ashurst (1 mile).

🚗 (80) CP D V S

Meon Valley Vineyard

Hill Grove, Swanmore, Southampton, Hampshire SO3 2PZ
☎ (0489) 877435
Contact: C J or K Hartley, Proprietors

Vineyard planted in 1977 producing and selling wines from 1984 including red, white and rosé. Also sparkling wines (methode Champenoise) and farmhouse cider. Tours and tastings (according to season). Visitors can see pruning, winemaking, bottling and harvesting. Guided tours (2 hrs).
Admission: By appointment (min notice 7 days). Suitable for individuals, families and groups of 10-40 people. Adults and OAPs £1.85, children free. 10% discount for parties of over 30 people. Products for sale and orders accepted. Bar.
Directions: From M27 take Swanmore via Shedfield. Vineyard next to Hunters Inn crossroads 2 miles further on. Nearest railway station: Fareham or Winchester (10 miles).

🚗 CP D S

Whitchurch

Whitchurch Silk Mill

28 Winchester Street, Whitchurch,
Hampshire RG28 7AL
☎ (0256) 892065
Contact: Mr W B Carr, General Manager

19th century working mill producing silk for academic gowns, theatrical costumes, shirts etc. Some machines powered by water. Silk woven on original looms, warping and winding gear. Situated in grounds by river Test. Tours (1 hr) preceded by a video on silk production.

Admission: Appointments not necessary for individuals but min notice 2 weeks for organised tours. Open all year Tue-Sun and Bank Holidays 10.30-17.00 hrs. Looms not working Sun. Last admission time 16.00 hrs. Suitable for individuals, families, school parties (age 9+) and groups of up to 50 people. Adults £1.50, OAPs £1, children 50p. Visitors can purchase goods from shop and orders accepted for products.

Directions: From A34 Newbury-Winchester road, take B3400 into Whitchurch. Mill ¼ mile from town centre on River Test. Nearest railway station: Whitchurch (1 mile).

🚗 CP V SB S

HEREFORD & WORCESTER

Worcester

Royal Worcester Limited

Severn Street, Worcester WR1 2NE
☎ (0905) 23221
Contact: Mrs P Savage, Tours Organiser

Founded in 1751, makers of high quality china and porcelain tableware, cookware, giftware and ornamental ware. Guided tours (1 hr) to watch the making and decorating of china and porcelain. Museum, shops.

Admission: Appointment not necessary but recommended. Factory tours starting 10.15 hrs all year (excl Public and Factory Holidays) Mon-Fri 09.30-17.00 hrs. Museum also open Sat 10.00-17.00 hrs. Suitable for individuals, families, school parties (age 8+) and groups. Adults £2.25, OAPs £2.25, children £1.25.

Directions: From M5 junct 7 follow signs for Worcester South to city centre. The factory is near Worcester Cathedral. Nearest railway and bus station: Worcester (½ mile).

🚗 (4) CP D R S

ISLE OF WIGHT

Yarmouth

Chessell Pottery (IOW) Limited

Chessell, Shalcombe, Nr Yarmouth,
Isle of Wight PO41 0UE
☎ (0983) 78248. Fax (0983) 78210
Contact: Mr J Francis, Managing Director

Creation of unique handmade decorative porcelain. Pottery housed in converted 300-year-old barn in the heart of the West Wight countryside. Visitors see all aspects of production incl casting, decorating and throwing (depending on time of visit). Staff happy to explain production processes. Shop.

Admission: No appointment necessary. Decorating studio open all year Mon-Fri 09.00-16.00 hrs (excl lunch break 12.30-13.00 hrs). Suitable for individuals, families, school parties (age 8+) and groups of up to 50 people (but only 25 people at a time inside pottery workshop). Adults and OAPs 20p, children 5p. No dogs, no smoking.

Directions: 7 miles from Newport on main Newport to Freshwater road at turning to Brook. Nearest bus station: Newport (7 miles).

🚗 (50) CP D S

ENGLAND

Heard on the Grapevine

Wine-making is confined to England and Wales, but it goes back at least to the time of the Romans, many of whose villas had vineyards attached. Vines were grown in Sussex at least seven centuries before the first grapes were planted in the Rheingau, Germany's main wine-growing region, but from the time of Henry VIII viticulture on a commercial basis fell into decline. Thanks to the initiative of a new generation of growers, however, Britain is today once again making its mark on the wine-lover's map.

EARLY VINEYARDS

Though they were ale-drinkers themselves, the Saxons who invaded our island in the sixth century found the Celts still enjoying their wine long after the last Romans had left. After the Norman conquest of 1066 a fair acreage of land was granted to French religious orders, who turned some of it over to the commercial cultivation of grapes. Domesday Book records some forty vineyards in Britain, some in what is now the heart of present-day London. A medieval map of the abbeys of England and Wales is, in effect, a guide to our most historic vineyards.

ENGLISH KINGS AND FRENCH CLARET

In 1152 the future King Henry II married Eleanor of Aquitaine and acquired for the crown the all-important wine-growing region of Bordeaux. Claret thus became indubitably 'English' and its popularity on our shores has remained undiminished ever since. With so much good wine readily available, our own small vineyards could not compete. The Black Death carved a grim swathe through the ranks of the labouring peasants on whom the growers depended, while the Dissolution of the Monasteries by Henry VIII removed the final vestiges of commercial wine-growing in this country. Occasionally enthusiasts would resurrect the old arts — in Victorian times the Marquis of Bute planted a fine vineyard at Castel Coch, near Cardiff — but vines themselves came to belong increasingly to the conservatory or cottage wall, regarded as little more than a curiosity in our climate.

GROWING NUMBERS

In fact there is no reason why grapes should not flourish in our southern counties, especially with the recent heatwave summers. The climate itself has not altered so very dramatically since Roman times, while horticultural science has increased by leaps and bounds. In the 1950s a few vineyards began to be planted, and by 1967 there were a couple of dozen, mostly in Kent, Sussex and Hampshire. Today that figure has grown to well over three hundred, and vineyards can be found at all points of the compass. Wisely, since our own tradition of wine-making effectively died out in the Middle Ages, the growers have started with a clean slate, studying grape varieties and production techniques from the established wine-growing regions to establish what would be best for Britain. And these first vintages have not merely been popular in the market-place — they have also proved themselves in competition against wines from all over the world. What finer tribute could there be to our revitalised wine-making industry?

KENT

ENGLAND

Ashford

Stevenson Brothers Rocking Horse Gallery & Workshop

The Workshop, Ashford Road, Bethersden, Ashford, Kent TN26 3AP
☎ (023 382) 363. Fax (023 38) 2580
Contact: Mr M Stevenson, Partner

Specialists in the making and restoration of traditional rocking-horses and carousel animals. Guided tours (½ hr) to see the making and carving of tiny toy horses and life-size sculptures involving woodworking processes and carving skills.
Admission: By written appointment for groups of 6+ people, by telephone for individuals and families. Open all year Mon-Fri 09.00-18.00 hrs, Sat by appointment only. Suitable for individuals, families, school parties (age 4+) and groups of up to 20 people. Adult groups £25 (min 20 people), school parties free. Products can be bought or orders taken.
Directions: On A28 between Ashford and Tenterden. Look for the horse on the roof. Nearest railway and bus station: Ashford (5 miles).

🚗 (12) CP S

Crayford

David Evans & Company

Bourne Road, Bourne Industrial Estate, Crayford, Kent, DA1 4BP
☎ (0322) 59401
Contact: Mrs B Ferguson, Marketing Co-ordinator

Old-established company since 1843, it is the last of the London textile printers. Discover the secrets of silk. Learn the fascinating history, techniques and sericulture and see the hand screen-printing and finishing of silk. Guided tours (1 hr), video (20 mins). Tours at 09.30, 11.00, 13.30 and 14.30 hrs.
Admission: No advance booking required for unguided tour of craft centre but 3/4 weeks in advance for guided tour. Open all year Mon-Fri 09.30-17.00 hrs, Sat 09.30-16.30 hrs. Closed Sun, Bank Holidays. Suitable for individuals, school parties (age 12+) and groups of 20-70 people. Adults £1.25, OAPs 75p.
Directions: M25 junct 2 then A2 to London. Exit Black Prince interchange signposted Bexley. Nearest railway station: Crayford (¾ mile). Nearest bus/coach station: Bexleyheath (½ mile).

🚗 (25) CP D SB S

Folkestone

Eurotunnel Exhibition Centre

St Martin's Plain, Cheriton High Street, Folkestone, Kent CT19 4QD
☎ (0303) 270111
Contact: Mr D Clapson, Exhibition Centre Mgr

Travel into the future. Models, maps, videos, games and displays explain how the tunnel will operate when open in 1993. 70ft viewing tower overlooking Cheriton Terminal site. Auditorium seating 80 people shows construction progress. Shop.
Admission: No appointment necessary. Open daily (except Monday) Mar-Oct 10.00-18.00 hrs, Oct-Mar 10.00-17.00 hrs incl Bank Holiday Mon. Suitable for individuals, families, school parties and groups. Adults £2.50, OAPs and children (under 16 yrs old) £1.50. Reduced rates for groups of 10+ people. No dogs except guide dogs.
Directions: Signs from M20, junct 12. Nearest railway and bus stations: Folkestone (4 miles).
See advertisement inside back cover.

🚗 CP D SB S

Lamberhurst

Lamberhurst Vineyards

Ridge Farm, Lamberhurst, Nr Tunbridge Wells, Kent TN3 8ER
☎ (0892) 890286
Contact: Mr T Pitcher, Mgr, Visitor Services

England's leading vineyard, producing fine English wines and liqueurs. Visitors can see harvesting (according to season), wine production and bottling. Guided tours (1½ hrs). 26 May-28 Oct 11.00-16.00 hrs. Tutored wine tastings available. Shop. Oasthouse 4 Conference and banqueting facilities. Own label wine produced.
Admission: No appointment necessary. Open in summer, Mon-Sat 09.00-18.00 hrs, Sun 10.00-17.00 hrs and in winter Mon-Sat 09.00-17.00 hrs. Sun 10.00-17.00 hrs. Suitable for individuals, families, school parties and groups of 15-56 people. Adults £1.95, OAPs and children (10-17 yrs) £1.45. Children under 10 free.
Directions: From M25 take A21 to Lamberhurst. Take right turn in village to Vineyard. Nearest railway and bus stations: Tunbridge Wells (6 miles).

🚗 CP S

Romney Marsh

Nuclear Electric

Dungeness Visitors Information Centre, Dungeness Power Station, Romney Marsh, Kent TN29 9PP
☎ (0679) 21815
Contact: Mr F Lang, Public Relations Officer

Guided tour (1½ hrs) of a working nuclear power station showing production of electricity. Various audio/video presentations in information centre.
Admission: Appointment necessary for tour but not for a visit to the information centre. Open every day in summer months 10.00-16.00 hrs, Mon-Sat in winter. Closed most Bank Holidays. Suitable for individuals, school parties (age 5+) and groups of up to 40 people. Max capacity 80 in centre. Free.
Directions: Off main A259 between Folkestone and Rye. Follow signs to Lydd then Dungeness. Nearest railway station: Ashford (22 miles). Nearest bus station: Lydd (5 miles). See advertisement page 11.

🚗 (40-60) CP V SB

LANCASHIRE

Blackpool

Coronation Rock Company Limited

11 Cherry Tree Road, North, Marton, Blackpool, Lancashire FY4 4NY
☎ (0253) 62366
Contact: Ms M Bell, General Office

Established in 1927 to produce traditional sugar confectionery to highest standards. Visitors watch production from a special viewing gallery. Also demonstrations of lettered rock-making and other hand-made specialised confectionery. Guided tours (45 mins).
Admission: No appointment necessary for individuals and families but min notice 2 days advisable for groups and school parties of 10-45 people. Suitable for children age 5+. Open all year (excl weekends and Public Holidays) Mon-Thur 09.00-15.30 hrs, Fri 09.00-12.00 hrs. Free. Orders taken for specially lettered rock sticks and sweets (complete boilings).
Directions: M55 junct 4 and then by A583 to Blackpool. Turn left at second set of traffic lights. The factory is about 100 yds further on left. Nearest railway stations: Blackpool South (1 mile), Blackpool North (2 miles).

🚗 (6) CP V S

ENGLAND

Bolton

Warburtons Limited

Bread Bakery, Hereford Street, Bolton, Lancashire BL1 8JB
☎ (0204) 23551
Contact: Mrs J Kippax, Public Relations Officer

One of the largest family-run bakeries in the country originating in Bolton over 100 years ago. Visitors see the making of high-quality bread products. Guided tour (1 ½ hrs) and video show (10 mins) at 14.30 and 19.30 hrs.
Admission: Appointment necessary (min notice 2 weeks). Open all year (excl Public Holidays) Tue and Thur 14.30 and 19.30 hrs, Wed 19.30 hrs. Suitable for individuals, families, school parties, groups and clubs (min age 14). Group sizes from 10-25 people. Free.
Directions: M61 junct 3 and then by A666. Nearest railway station: Bolton Trinity Street (2 miles). Nearest bus station: Moor Lane (2 miles).
🚗 CP

Carnforth

Carnforth Railway Restoration and Engineering Services

Warton Road, Carnforth, Lancashire LA5 9HX
☎ (0524) 734708
Contact: Mr N Tyhurst, Director

CRRES first formed in 1978 to build Orient Express. Have fulfilled many contracts since incl 15" miniature carriages for Japan and the luxury train Queen of Scots. Visitors can see work on various vehicles incl old railway carriages, steam engines, road transport.
Admission: Guided tours by appointment only (min notice 24 hrs). Open all year Mon-Thur 08.00-16.30 hrs, Fri 08.00-15.30 hrs, Sat & Sun by arrangement. Last admission 16.00 hrs. Suitable for individuals, families, school parties and groups. Static days: adults £1.50, OAPs and children 95p; miniature days: adults £2, children £1.35; full operating steam days: adults £2.80, children £1.90. Special reductions for groups and families.
Directions: From M6 junct 35 follow signs. Nearest railway station: Carnforth (¾ mile). Nearest bus station: Lancaster (6 miles).
🚗 (50) CP D V R SB

Morecambe

Nuclear Electric

Heysham Power Station, Information Centre, PO Box 17, Morecambe, Lancashire LA3 2YB
☎ (0524) 55624
Contact: Mrs J Moore, Information Officer

Guided tour (2½ hrs incl introductory video) of turbine hall, reactor viewing gallery and central control room involved in the generation of electricity using nuclear fission to produce heat.
Admission: No appointment necessary for tours for individuals and groups which start at 13.30 hrs. Groups of 10-16 people by appointment only. Information centre open Mon-Fri 1 Oct-31 Mar 10.00-16.00 hrs, 1 Apr-30 Sept 10.00-17.00 hrs, Sat and Sun 13.30-17.00 hrs. Closed 25, 26 Dec. Suitable for individuals, school parties and groups. Max capacity 200 people. Free. No recording equipment, pets or hand baggage. No unaccompanied children under age 14.
Directions: M6 junct 34, then follow to Morecambe A589. Nearest railway station: Morecambe Promenade (3 miles). Nearest coach station: Morecambe Poulton Square (4 miles). Bus to within ½ mile.
See advertisement page 11
🚗 (80) CP D V SB

Preston

Whitbread and Company plc

The Brewery, Cuerdale Lane, Samlesbury, Nr Preston, Lancashire PR5 0XD
☎ (0772) 877681
Contact: Mrs R Hodson, Public Relations Offr.

A modern brewery built on a green field site where visitors can see beer production from raw materials through to final packaging. Guided tours (2-3 hrs) at 11.00 and 19.30 hrs. Video.
Admission: By appointment only. Open Jan-Nov Mon-Thur (excl Public Holidays). Suitable for groups of 25 people. £75 per group booking of 25 people (incl refreshments).
Directions: 5 mins from junct 31 on M6. Take A677 towards Blackburn for approx 2 miles then take B6320 Walton-le-Dale prior to junct with A59 signposted Skipton. Brewery on right. Nearest railway and bus station: Preston (5 miles).

CP V

LEICESTERSHIRE

Loughborough

John Taylor Bellfoundry and Museum

Freehold Street, Loughborough, Leicestershire LE11 1AR
☎ (0509) 233414
Contact: Mr T S Jennings, Curator

200-year-old bellfounding complex incl museum. The largest working bellfoundry in the world. Visitors see all aspects of bellfoundry. Guided tours (approx 45 mins) are compulsory and show work progressing in the bellfoundry.
Admission: No appointment necessary for museum but min notice 2 days for tour. Open all year Tue-Sat and Bank Holiday Mon 09.30-12.30 hrs and 13.30-16.30 hrs. Last admission 16.00 hrs. Suitable for individuals (museum only), school parties (age 6+) and groups of 15-100 people. Adults £2 (museum only 75p), OAPs £2, children £1, (museum only 50p). No animals incl guide dogs. Visitors can purchase goods from shop. Orders accepted for all forms of bells.
Directions: Leave M1 at junct 23 then A512 and A6. Signposted in Loughborough. Nearest railway station: Loughborough main line (1000 m). Nearest bus/coach station: Loughborough (800 m).

D S

LONDON

Lloyd's of London

1 Lime Street, London EC3M 7HA
☎ 071-623 7100
Contact: Miss D Boyden, Manager, Visitors Exhibition

International insurance market originating over 300 years ago in Edward Lloyd's coffee house. Now located in the architecturally stunning Richard Rogers building. From the gallery visitors can see brokers travelling on illuminated escalators between floors of underwriters. Lively exhibition of how Lloyd's works. Assistants available who can speak several European languages. Shop.
Admission: No appointment necessary for individuals or small groups of up to 8 people. Min notice 1 week for groups of 8-20 people (min age 6+) subject to availability. Open Mon-Fri 10.00-14.30 hrs (15.45 hrs for pre-booked groups). Closed 24 Dec-1 Jan and Public Holidays. Suitable for individuals, families, school parties and groups. Free.
Directions: River bus to Swan Lane Pier. Nearest railway/tube stations: Fenchurch Street, Liverpool Street, London Bridge, Bank or Monument.

D (by arrangement) V S

Establishments who have confirmed that they have suitable facilities for disabled people are shown with this symbol.

ENGLAND

The London Diamond Centre

10 Hanover Street, London W1R 9HF
☎ 071-629 5511
Contact: Mr M L Prince, Marketing Manager

A fully guided tour (approx 40 mins) of a unique diamond exhibition where you can see diamond polishers practising their craft, a video of diamond mining and many other aspects of the diamond industry. Visitors given an in depth explanation and can browse around one of the largest jewellery showrooms in the world. Diamonds and jewellery can be purchased at factory prices (tax free for overseas visitors).
Admission: No appointment necessary. Open all year Mon-Fri 09.30-17.30 hrs, Sat 09.30-13.30 hrs. Suitable for individuals, families and groups of 10-50 people. £3.45 (incl free brilliant cut stone but not a diamond which visitors may have set in mounting of their choice). The management reserves the right to refuse admission.
Directions: Located in London's West End. Hanover Street is off Regent Street. Nearest tube station: Oxford Circus (3 mins walk). Nearest bus station: Victoria (10 mins by tube).

London Docklands Development Corporation

Visitor Centre, 3 Limeharbour, London E14 9TJ
☎ 071-515 300
Contact: Ms H Watters, Tourism Development Executive

London Docklands is a dynamic re-development area of 8½ sq miles north and south of the River Thames. Visitors can see the regeneration of the area. Tours (2 hrs) by appointment. Audio-visual presentation.
Admission: Appointment required (min notice 1 week). Suitable for individuals, families, school parties (age 12+) and groups of 10-100 people. Tours from about £40 per group (depending on size of group).
Directions: Off A13 travelling east out of Central London. Nearest railway station: Cross Harbour (Docklands Light Railway).
See advertisement page 13

🚗 (30) CP D V

Telecom Technology Showcase

135 Queen Victoria Street, London EC4V 4AT
☎ 071-248 7444 (main office), 071-248 7447 (Resource Centre), 0800 289698 (free information line)
Contact: Ms J Ely, Administrator

British Telecom's award-winning museum reflects the profound influence of telecommunications over 150 years. From the first telegraphs and telephones to today's information revolution, this fascinating history is told using many working models and exhibits, with supporting videos and sound effects. Showcase also includes a shop, lecture theatre seating 35-40 persons, and 'Resource Centre' for historical research, with journal, document, photograph and telephone directory collections. Visits (1 hr) to Resource Centre by appointment.
Admission: No advance appointment necessary for individuals and families (excl Resource Centre) but advance booking essential for school parties (age 8+) and groups of 10-50 people. Open all year Mon-Fri 10.00-17.00 hrs (excl Public Holidays). Open on Lord Mayor's Show Day in Nov. Free. Shop.
Directions: Queen Victoria Street leads from Bank to Blackfriars Bridge. Nearest railway station: Blackfriars (tube, BR) adjacent. Parking (100 yds) at NCP car park. Coach parking at St Pauls (½ mile).

V S

Thames Barrier Visitors Centre

Unity Way, Woolwich, London SE18 5NJ
☎ 081-854 1373
Contact: Mr J Hawkins, Visitor Centre Mgr

At a cost of £500m, the 6-year-old Barrier is the largest movable flood barrier in the world, spanning ⅓ mile across the River Thames. Visitors can see monthly 2½ hr test closure or annual all-day full tidal closure of all gates. Multi-media audio visual show, working model, occasional organised tours for technical groups or optional ½ hr boat trip. Shop.
Admission: No appointment necessary but groups advised to give advance notice wherever possible. Open all year Mon-Fri 10.30-17.00 hrs, Sat and Sun 10.30-17.30 hrs. Closed Christmas and Bank Holidays. Suitable for individuals, families, school parties (age 6+) and groups. Adults £2, OAPs and children £1.20, family ticket (up to 5 people) £5.50. Reduced price for groups of 20+ people.
Directions: Cross River Thames (north to south) by Blackwall Tunnel or Woolwich Ferry (free). Signposted from A206 Woolwich Road. Nearest railway station: Charlton (1 mile). Nearest coach station: Victoria (5 miles).

🚗 (250) CP D V R SB S

Tower Bridge

London SE1 2UP
☎ 071-407 0922
Contact: Mr M Waters, Tourism Manager

This world famous bridge still performs its original task of lifting in order to enable ships to enter the Pool of London (it was opened 500 times in 1989). Several exhibitions within structure, original Victorian steam engines, panoramic views of London. Video giving brief history and showing bridge lift.
Admission: No appointment necessary. Open daily 1 Nov-31 Mar 10.00-16.45 hrs, 1 Apr-31 Oct 10.00-18.30 hrs. Last tickets sold 45 mins before close. Bridge closed New Year's Day, Good Friday, Christmas Eve, Christmas Day and Boxing Day. Suitable for individuals, families, school parties and groups of 10-100 people. Adults £2.50, OAPs and children £1. Special reduced group rates (adults) £2 (£2.25 in Jul/Aug). Shop open during Bridge opening hours.
Directions: Underground to Tower Hill or London Bridge. Numerous buses stop nearby.

D

The Wimbledon Lawn Tennis Museum

The All England Club, Church Road, Wimbledon, London SW19 5AE
☎ 081-946 6131
Contact: Mrs Newell, Museum Secretary

Museum displays trace the development of lawn tennis from a polite Victorian pastime to the lucrative professional sport seen today. From mid-Aug to mid-May visitors can see videos showing highlights of the championships 11.00-17.00 hrs. View over Centre Court. Racquet-makers' workshop. Shop.
Admission: No appointment necessary. Open all year Tue-Sat 11.00-17.00 hrs, Sun 14.00-17.00 hrs. Closed Mon, Public and Bank Holidays. Christmas/New Year details on request. Open only to spectators during championships. Suitable for individuals, families, groups and school parties (age 7+). Adults £1.50, OAPs and children (under 16) 75p. 10% reduction for groups of 20-50 booked in advance.
Directions: Nearest railway station: Southfields (District line tube) or Wimbledon BR (1 mile).

🚗 (15+) CP D S

ENGLAND

ENGLAND

MERSEYSIDE

Port Sunlight

Port Sunlight Heritage Centre

PO Box 139, Greendale Road, Port Sunlight, Wirral, Merseyside L62 4ZP
☎ 051-644 6466
Contact: Ms K Gilfoyle, Information Officer

Port Sunlight Heritage Centre tells the story of how over 100 yrs ago William Lever set up his famous soap factory and model garden village. Displays of soap packaging, period advertising and a model of the village. Guided tours (30-45 mins) can be arranged in advance for coach parties. Guides will board coaches (£10 fee to be paid in advance).
Admission: No appointment necessary except for large parties. Open Easter to end-Oct daily 12.00-16.00 hrs, Nov-Easter Mon-Fri 12.00-16.00 hrs. Last admission time 15.45 hrs. Suitable for individuals, families, school parties and groups of up to 56 people. Adults and OAPs 20p, children free. Coach parties free. No unaccompanied children.
Directions: From M56 junct 4, take B5137. Port Sunlight village is signposted. Nearest railway station: Port Sunlight (100 yds).

MIDDLESEX

Edgware

Boosey & Hawkes Musical Instruments Limited

Deansbrook Road, Edgware, Middlesex HA8 9BB
☎ 081-952 7711
Contact: Ms D Mooney, Advertising & Promotions Asst

Manufacturers of band and orchestral musical instruments. Part of the Boosey & Hawkes Group, the factory has been at Edgware since 1924. Visitors can see the complete manufacturing process of brass musical instruments and flutes plus museum. Guided tours (1½-2 hrs) at 10.00 or 14.00 hrs (Wed only).
Admission: By appointment only with the min notice of 3/4 weeks. Suitable for individuals, groups and school parties of up to 35 people. Suitable for children age 11+.

Adults, OAPs and children 50p. Promotional items can be bought (sweatshirts, ties etc.)
Directions: M1 junct 4 and A5 to central London. Nearest tube station: Edgware Station on Northern Line (10 mins walk).

🚗 CP R (by arrangement) S

Uxbridge

Park Lodge Farm Centre

Harvil Road, Harefield, Uxbridge, Middlesex UB8 1NJ
☎ (0895) 824425 (answerphone)
Contact: Mrs Shepherd
☎ (0895) 31949 Ext 407

A commercial agricultural enterprise, managed by the London Borough of Hillingdon, where groups studying farming or other countryside matters can see a 700-acre dairy and sheep farm, seasonal agricultural activities and daily milking routine.
Admission: By appointment (min notice 2 weeks). Open every day of school term only during normal school hours. Suitable for school parties of up to 150 (age 5+). £27 per party of 50 children.
Directions: From M25 to M4 (Uxbridge turn off), then A40 and follow signs to Harefield. Nearest railway station: Denham (2 miles). Nearest bus station: Uxbridge (4 miles).

🚗 (20) CP V

NORFOLK

Dereham

Norfolk Rural Life Museum

Beech House, Gressenhall, Dereham,
Norfolk NR20 4DR
☎ (0362) 860563
Contact: Ms B Yates, Curator

Working life in the past shown through reconstructed craft workshops (saddler, blacksmith, wheelwright, baker, seed merchant, basket-maker, village shop). Working 1920s farm with local rare breeds. Nature trail. Demonstrations on Sun — programme available. Shop.
Admission: No appointment necessary. Open Easter Sun-28 Oct Tue-Sat 10.00-17.00 hrs, Sun 14.00-17.30 hrs, Bank Holiday Mon 10.00-17.00 hrs. Suitable for individuals, families, groups and school parties. Adults £2, OAPs £1.75, children 60p. Groups of 10+ people £1.50.
Directions: Off A47 on to B1110. Turn on to B1146 and signposted from there. Nearest railway station: Norwich (21 miles). Nearest bus station: Dereham (3 miles).

(200) CP D R SB S

King's Lynn

Caithness Crystal Limited

Oldmeadow Road, Hardwick Industrial Estate,
King's Lynn, Norfolk PE30 4JT
☎ (0553) 765111
Contact: Mrs D Johnson, Visitor Service Mgr

Modern factory making crystal glassware in the manner it has been made for centuries. Marvel at the skills of the glassmaker as he fashions molten glass into goblets, decanters and vases. Craftsmen finish and hand-cut the crystal glass. Guided tours (30 mins). Glass-making demonstrations at weekends. Shop.
Admission: By appointment only all year Mon-Fri 09.30-16.00 hrs, weekends 27 May-16 Sept 11.00-16.00 hrs. Open Bank Holidays (excl Good Friday, Christmas/New Year). Suitable for families, individuals, school parties (ages 6-18) and groups of 2-60 people. Adults £1, children 50p. Reductions for groups of 10+ people.
Directions: Signposted on A10, A47 and A149 on approaches to King's Lynn. Nearest railway and bus station: King's Lynn (3 miles).

(60) CP SB S

NORTHUMBERLAND

Alnwick

House of Hardy Limited

Willowburn, Alnwick, Northumberland
NE66 2PG
☎ (0665) 602771
Contact: Mr M Hennessey, Countrystore Manager

Museum, Countrystore and factory offer the chance to see in the making the finest quality game fishing tackle using both techniques dating back to 1872 and those of the present day. Production of rods and reels using traditional skills in tandem with high technology. Guided tours (1½ hrs) Mon-Thur 10.00 and 14.00 hrs, Fri 10.00 hrs.
Admission: Factory tours by appointment only (min notice 1 day). Open Mon-Fri 09.00-17.00 hrs, Sat 10.00-17.00 hrs, Sun (Mar-Oct incl) 13.30-17.00 hrs. Last admission 17.00 hrs. Factory tours suitable for individuals, groups and school parties of up to 6 people. Age 16+ unless accompanied by an adult. Free. Products for sale in shop.
Directions: From the north take second exit to Alnwick, through underpass and right at crossroads (300 yds). From the south, take first exit to Alnwick, 400 yds on right. Nearest railway station: Alnmouth (3 miles). Nearest bus station: Alnwick (1 mile). Buses stop outside.

CP D S

Establishments who have confirmed that they have suitable facilities for disabled people are shown with this symbol.

ENGLAND

Belford

Norselands Gallery Studio Two

The Old School, Warenford, Nr Belford, Northumberland NE70 7HY
☎ (0668) 213465
Contact: Mr B & Mrs V Rawlinson, Partners/Owners

Family-run business featuring the 'best of British' crafts galley and ceramic workshop in attractive old school. Pleasant rural setting with bonsai house and aviary. Visitors can see hand-crafted ceramic figures, children, fantasy pieces and fungi planters in the making.
Admission: No appointment necessary. Open all year (excl Christmas) every day 09.00-21.00 hrs in summer season, 09.00-17.00 hrs in winter season. Free. Evening demonstrations 19.00-21.00 hrs. Group bookings taken for evening with min charge of £10 for up to 20 people. Max capacity 30 people. No unaccompanied children under 10 yrs old. Shop. Special pieces made to order.
Directions: On A1 10 miles north of Alnwick, 2½ miles south of Belford. Look for official sign on A1 'Craft Gallery Workshop'. Nearest railway station: Berwick (18 miles). Nearest bus/coach station: Alnwick (10 miles).

🚗 (10) CP SB S

Otterburn

Redesdale Dairy

Soppitt Farm, Otterburn, Northumberland NE19 1AF
☎ (0830) 20506
Contact: Mr M Robertson, Owner

The hand-making of farmhouse cheese from cow's, sheep's and goat's milk. Video on cheesemaking, discussion and tour (40 mins). Products can be bought.
Admission: Appointments necessary only for groups of 15-40 people. Farm shop open daily Easter-Oct 10.00-17.30 hrs, Oct-Easter 10.00-14.00 hrs. Tea room open Easter-Oct only. Suitable for individuals, families, groups and school parties (age 8+). Prices from £2.
Directions: 2 miles east of Otterburn on B6341. Follow sign at junct of A696/B6341. Nearest bus station: Otterburn (2 miles).

🚗 (20) CP D SB S

SOMERSET

Bridgwater

Nuclear Electric plc

Energy Information Centre, Hinkley Point Power Station, Bridgwater, Somerset TA5 1UD
☎ (0278) 653492 Information Centre; (0278) 652461 Power Station
Contact: Mrs J Goodchild, Senior Information Officer or Mrs J Lucas, Visits Organiser.

A working power station with information centre and Educational Resource Centre. Presentations to groups on special topics are available on request either at Information Centre or venue of your choice. Curriculum material for teacher's study programmes available. Guided tours (2 hrs) at 10.30, 14.30 and 19.30 hrs.
Admission: By appointment only (48 hrs notice required). Open all year (excl Public Holidays). Last admission 16.00 hrs. Suitable for individuals, families, groups and school parties (age 9+) of up to 40 people. Larger parties can be accommodated by prior arrangement. Free.
Direction: M5 junct 23, A39 to Cannington, turn right at War Memorial towards Hinkley Point. Nearest railway and bus station: Bridgwater (11 miles).
See advertisement page 11.

🚗 CP D V

Ilchester

Fleet Air Arm Museum

Royal Naval Air Station, Yeovilton, Nr Ilchester, Somerset BA22 8HT
☎ (0935) 840565
Contact: Ms J Hodgkins, Publicity Officer

One of the world's major aviation museums with more than 50 historic aircraft on display including Concorde 002. A working museum with all aspects of museum maintenance on view, construction of exhibitions, the day-to-day running etc. No guided tours organised. Short talk with audio-visual presentation.
Admission: By appointment (min notice 2/3 days). Open all year (excl 24-26 Dec) 10.00-17.30 hrs in summer, 10.00-16.30 hrs in winter. Suitable for individuals, families, school parties and groups of 15+ people. Adults £3.70, OAPs £3, children £2. Reduced rates for groups. Shop and restaurant.
Directions: Off the A303/A37 nr Ilchester on the B3151, 7 miles from Yeovil. Nearest railway and bus stations: Yeovil (7 miles).

🚗 CP D V R SB S

Minehead

John Wood & Sons (Exmoor) Limited

Old Cleeve, Minehead, Somerset TA24 6HT
☎ (0984) 40291
Contact: Mrs P Scragg, Office Manager

For over 100 years John Wood has processed sheepskins into high quality, handcrafted products. Bargain items include moccasins, flying jackets and toys. Watch sheepskins crafted into slippers, coats and rugs from dyeing to stitching. Guided tours (1 hr). Video and demonstrations of work.
Admission: No appointment required for individuals and small groups but advance notice necessary for large parties. Tours available Easter-Oct Mon-Fri at 10.45, 11.30, 14.15 and 15.00 hrs. Suitable for individuals, families, school parties (ages 8-16) and groups of up to 25 people. Free. Craft shop open all year Mon-Fri 09.00-17.00 hrs, Sat & Public Holidays 10.00-16.00 hrs.
Directions: On A39 Minehead to Williton road 6 miles east of Washford. Nearest railway and bus stations: Minehead.

🚗 (200) CP D S

Shepton Mallet

North Wootton Vineyard

North Wootton, Shepton Mallet, Somerset BA4 4AG
☎ (074 989) 359
Contact: Major Gillespie, Winegrower

6 acres of vines planted in 1971. A working vineyard. Guided tours (1¼ hrs incl tasting).
Admission: No appointment necessary (except for guided tours). Open all year daily 10.00-13.00 hrs, 14.00-17.00 hrs. Closed Sun. Suitable for individuals, families, school parties and groups of 20-45 people. Adults £3.25 incl wine tasting. Sale of products as times above.
Directions: Clearly signposted from A361 between Glastonbury and Shepton Mallet.

🚗 (50) CP S

STAFFORDSHIRE

Burton-on-Trent

Bass Museum, Visitor Centre and Shire Horse Stables

Bass Brewing, Horninglow Street, Burton-on-Trent, Staffordshire DE14 1JZ
☎ (0283) 45301 (until Aug 1990 then 511000)
Contact: Ms G McBride, Museum Administrator

A museum which preserves and presents the story of Bass, Britain's premier brewer. Home of the famous Bass Shire Horse team. Guided tour of brewery (1 hr) and audio-visuals throughout museum.
Admission: Appointment necessary for brewery tour (must be age 14+). Open Mon-Fri 10.00-17.00 hrs, Sat and Sun 10.30-17.00 hrs. Last admission 16.00 hrs. Suitable for individuals, families, groups and school parties. Reduced rates for groups of up to 52 people. Adults £2.75 (incl ½ pt sample), OAPs £1.75 (museum only), children £1.25 (museum only). Special rates for educational visits. Special arrangements for brewery tours. Shop and licensed bar. Orders taken for specialised bottles of beer.
Directions: On main A50 in Burton. Nearest train/bus stations: Burton-on-Trent.

🚗 (100+) CP R SB S

ENGLAND

Going to pot

Britain's potteries have a reputation that extends all around the world, whether it is for fine bone china from the famous ceramics factories or the skilled hand-crafted work of our artist-potters. All over the country you can see pottery made, and follow every stage of the process.

TRADITION AND TECHNOLOGY

Pottery is made by a variety of different techniques. You can still feel the magic as a pot is created on a wheel, watching the potter impose his or her own personality on the work by the way it is shaped, decorated and glazed. This is how, in essence, all pottery was made at one time, from ancient times right up until the Industrial Revolution, when the first generation of pottery factories was established.

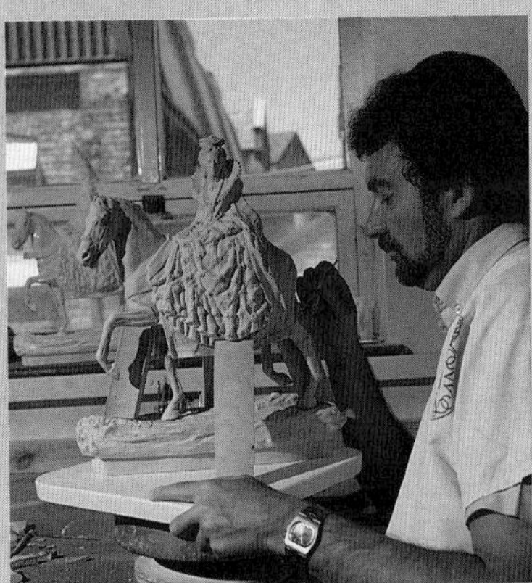

THE INDIVIDUAL TOUCH

The production of pottery on an industrial scale is an equally fascinating process to watch. At many of the places listed in this guide you can follow the sequence from start to finish, from preparing the clay right through to glazing and firing. Almost all actually sell the goods you have seen produced, and many offer 'seconds'—just the thing for bargain-hunters. All potteries are proud of the distinctive stamp they give their work, and many have evolved special production methods to give their products a character all their own. But the old skills still live on, however, and in many factories—just as in potters' studios—you will be aware of the exquisite care that goes into shaping and finishing, a reminder of how often in Britain tradition and technology are joined in the quest for perfection.

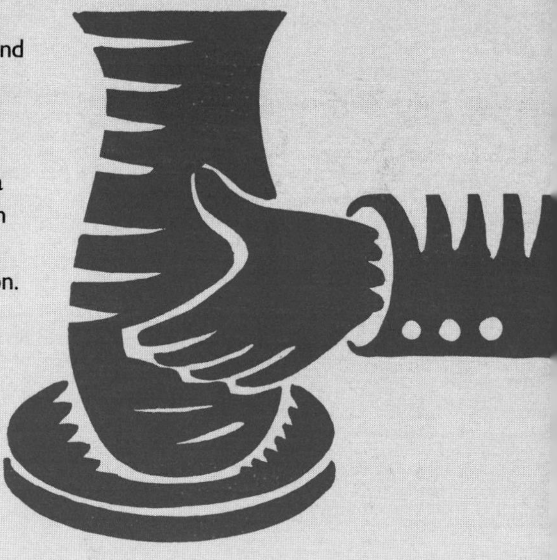

Tutbury Crystal Glass Limited

Burton Street, Tutbury, Burton-on-Trent, Staffordshire DE13 9NG
☎ (0283) 813281
Contact: Mrs S Ward, Reception

Hand-made, hand-decorated full lead crystal glass manufactured on a site where glassware has been made for approx 250 yrs. Guided tour (1 hr) to see all stages of manufacture. Demonstrations at 09.30, 11.30 and 15.30 hrs on Mon, Tue, Thur and Fri.
Admission: By appointment only (min notice 7 days). Open all year (except Christmas/New Year). Open to groups of 12-60 people and school parties (age 10+). 20p. Full range of glassware on sale. Orders accepted.
Directions: On the A50 5 miles from Burton-on-Trent. Nearest railway station: Tutbury (½ mile). On bus routes.

🚗 (15) CP D SB S

Leek

Cheddleton Flint Mill

Leek Road, Cheddleton, Nr Leek, Staffordshire
☎ (078 139) 2561
Contact: Mr R Copeland, Secretary Briton House, Tittensor, Stoke on Trent, Staffordshire ST12 9HH
☎ (078 139) 2561

Twin water-wheels situated on River Churnet which have driven flint grinding pans since 1800. Visitors can see Robey steam engine and 'Vienna' a narrowboat moored on Caldon Canal. Tours available (1 hr).
Admission: No appointment necessary except for guided tours where min notice of 3 weeks required. Open all year Mon-Fri 10.00-17.30 hrs, weekends pm only. Last admission time 17.00 hrs. Suitable for individuals, families, groups and school parties of up to 50 people. Free (but donations very welcome).
Directions: On A520 between Stoke-on-Trent and Leek on west side of road in valley. Nearest railway station: Stoke-on-Trent (12 miles). Nearest bus station: Hanley (10 miles).

🚗 D

Stoke-on-Trent

Etruria Industrial Museum

Lower Bedford Street, Etruria, Stoke-on-Trent, Staffordshire ST4 7AF
☎ (0782) 287557
Contact: Ms A Nuttall, Assistant Keeper

Britain's sole surviving steam powered potter's mill. The Etruscan bone and flint mill ground materials for the agricultural and pottery industries from 1857-1972. Visitors can see the grinding pans, gears, flint kiln, boiler and engine of the mill. Guided tours (1 hr). Demonstrations of steam operated pulsometer pump, horizontal engine, crusher & beam engine at 10.00, 11.30, 14.00 hrs.
Admission: No appointment necessary. Open all year Wed-Sun 10.00-16.00 hrs. Last admission 16.00 hrs. Suitable for individuals, families, school parties (ages 5-18) and groups of up to 25 people. Free.
Directions: From M6 junct 15 take A500, then A53 (direction Hanley/Leek). Take right at Festival Park roundabout. Nearest railway station: Stoke-on-Trent (¾ mile). Nearest bus station: Hanley (¾ mile).

🚗 (60) CP V

Royal Doulton

Minton House, London Road, Stoke-on-Trent, Staffordshire ST4 7QD
☎ (0782) 744766
Contact: Mr J Morton, Tours Officer

Manufacturers of fine bone china. Guided tours of 5 working factories: Royal Doulton, Royal Crown Derby, Minton, John Beswick and Royal Doulton Crystal. Visitors see all stages in the production of fine bone china and finest English crystal. Guided tours (1 hr) at 10.30 and 14.00 hrs. Museum, shops open all day.
Admission: Appointment not necessary but advised. Open all year Mon-Fri (closed factory holidays). Factory shops open all year Mon-Sat 09.00-17.30 hrs. Suitable for individuals, families, school parties (age 14+) and groups of 30-70 people. Adults £2, OAPs and children £1.50. Reduced rates for groups (min 30 people). Catering available on pre-booked basis only. Products can be bought. Orders accepted for UK and overseas.
Directions: From M6 junct 15, take A500. Signs from there. Nearest railway station: Stoke on Trent (1 mile). Regular bus service.

🚗 CP S

Royal Grafton China

Grafton Works, Marlborough Road, Longton, Stoke-on-Trent, Staffordshire ST3 1ED
☎ (0782) 599667
Contact: Ms A Bentley, Factory Shop Mgress

Originally established in 1876, Royal Grafton China are one of the leading manufacturers of fine bone china tableware and giftware, supplying both the home and export markets. Guided tour (1 hr) — visitors see the manufacture of china from clay stage to finished product.
Admission: By appointment (min notice 2 days). Open all year (incl Bank Holidays and Factory Holidays) Mon-Fri 09.00-16.30 hrs, Sat 09.00-15.00 hrs. Closed Christmas/New Year. Suitable for individuals, and groups of 30-50 people. Adults £1, OAPs and groups 75p. 'Seconds' on sale in shop at reduced prices.
Directions: From M6 junct 15, take Queensway to first roundabout and Longton is signposted from there. Nearest railway station: Stoke-on-Trent (4 miles). Nearest bus station: Longton (¼ mile).

🚗 (6) SB S

Spode

Church Street, Stoke-on-Trent, Staffordshire ST4 1BX
☎ (0782) 744011. Contact: Tours Organiser

Manufacturers of high quality fine bone china, earthenware, stoneware and giftware. Established in 1770 as the birthplace of the fine bone china and the perfection of under-glaze printing technique. Visitors can see the manufacturing and decorating of tableware and giftware and tour the famous Spode Museum and Blue Room. Guided tours (standard tour 1¾ hrs, connoisseur 2½ hrs) Mon-Thur at 10.00 and 14.00 hrs, Fri at 10.00 hrs only. Shop. Orders accepted.
Admission: By appointment (min notice 24 hrs). Open all year (excl Christmas and Bank Holidays). Tour (times as above). Shop open Mon-Thur 09.00-17.00 hrs, Fri and Sat 09.00-16.00 hrs. Suitable for individuals, school parties (age 12+) and groups of up to 50 people. Adults, OAPs and children £1.25.
Directions: From M6 junct 15 take A500. Go over flyover and then first left at roundabout in centre of Stoke. Follow 'Heritage Trail' signs for Spode. Nearest railway station: Stoke-on-Trent (¼ mile). Nearest bus station: Hanley (2 miles).

🚗 CP R SB S

Staffordshire Enamels Limited

Cinderhill Industrial Estate, West Ceyney Road, Longton, Stoke-on-Trent, Staffordshire ST3 5ET
☎ (0782) 599948
Contact: Mrs Edna Dean, Customer Liaison

Privately owned specialist manufacturers of a range of hand-painted enamels making boxes and other decorative accessories — the revival of a lost art. Visitors can see enamelling, hand painting and final inspection assembly. Guided tour available (15 mins or longer if required).
Admission: Appointment necessary (minimum notice 1 day). Open all year (excl Public Holidays and Christmas/New Year) Mon-Fri 09.00-17.00 hrs. Last admission 16.00 hrs. Suitable for individuals, families, school parties and groups of up to 10 people. Free. Shop where seconds and discontinued ranges sold.
Directions: From M6 junct 15, follow signs for Stoke-on-Trent and Longton. Nearest railway station: Stoke-on-Trent (4 miles). Nearest bus station: Hanley (5 miles).

🚗 (6) CP SB S

Wedgwood Visitor Centre

Barlaston, Nr Stoke-on-Trent, Staffordshire ST12 9ES
☎ (0782) 204141/204218
Contact: Mr M Peddar, Manager

Audio-visual show and living museum illustrating 300 yrs of company history. Art gallery, demonstration hall, shop. Visitors can see throwing at potter's wheel and hand-painting of bone china.
Admission: No appointment required. Open all year incl Bank Holidays (excl Christmas/New Year) Mon-Fri 09.00-17.00 hrs, Sat 10.00-16.00 hrs plus Sun 10.00-16.00 hrs (Easter-Oct only). Suitable for individuals, families, school parties (age 5+) and groups. Adults £2, OAPs and children £1.25, groups of 12+ people £1.25.
Directions: From M6 take exit 14 or 15. Take A34 to Tittensor, then follow signs. Nearest railway station: Stoke (6 miles). Nearest bus station: Hanley (8 miles).
See advertisement page 14

🚗 (100) D SB S

ENGLAND

ENGLAND

SUFFOLK

Beccles

Winter Flora Limited

Hall Farm, Weston, Beccles, Suffolk NR34 8TT
☎ (0502) 713346
Contact: Ms P Veale, Secretary, or
Ms J Seppings, Director

40 acres of flowers and grasses grown on Company farms in the Waveney Valley. These are dried and arranged into posies, baskets, garlands and wreaths. Visitors can see flower arranging in the flower barn.

Admission: No appointment necessary except for groups of 7-40 people. Open all year (excl Public Holidays) Mon-Fri 09.00-17.00 hrs. Closed 13.00-14.00 hrs. Last admission 16.00 hrs. Free. Products can be bought from flower barn. Orders accepted. Customers may bring own containers for arrangements to be supplied to their specifications, colour etc.

Directions: Approx 1 mile south of Beccles on A145. Nearest railway station: Wickham Market (5 miles).

🚗 CP (by arrangement) S

Framlingham

James White Suffolk Cider

The Cider House, Friday Street,
Nr Framlingham, Suffolk IP13 7BP
☎ (072 882) 537
Contact: Mrs D Dale, Customer Relations

Makers of traditional ciders, fine apple juices and cider vinegar produced from freshly-pressed English apples and matured in oak casks. Guided tours (20 mins) daily during the season (Sept-June) to watch pressing and bottling.

Admission: No appointment necessary Mon-Fri 09.00-17.00 hrs but by appointment only at weekends (min notice 24 hrs). Suitable for individuals, families, school parties and groups of 10-100 people. Free. Cases can be ordered.

Directions: From Earl Soham on A1120 follow signs to Brandeston. Turn right opposite Queen's Head pub and right at T junct. After ½ mile take first left. Cider House 150 yds on right. Nearest railway/bus station: Wickham Market (5 miles).

🚗 (20) CP S

Newmarket

Newmarket Equine Tours

National Horseracing Museum,
99 High Street, Newmarket, Suffolk CB8 8JL
☎ (0638) 667333
Contact: Mr J L Round-Turner, Director

Visits to working training yard and stud to see exercise on gallops, thoroughbred training, stable and stud operation. Museum illustrates history of horseracing. Guided tours (4 hrs). Video of foal's birth at national stud. Gift shop.
Admission: By appointment only (min notice 2 days). Open Apr-Oct Tue-Sat. Tours at 09.30 hrs to training establishment and stud, 13.15 hrs stud only plus historic tour. Suitable for individuals, families, school parties and groups age (11+). Groups of 20-50 people. Adults £14.95 (£6.95 afternoons only), OAPs and children £10.95 (£4.50 afternoons only). Reduced group rates £2 discount per person (£1 afternoons). Gift shop open Tue-Sat 10.00-17.00 hrs.
Directions: Newmarket High Street, next to the Jockey Club. Nearest railway station: Newmarket (½ mile). Nearest bus/coach station: Newmarket (20 yds).

🚗 (100) CP D SB S

Leiston

Sizewell Information Centre

Sizewell B Site, Nr Leiston, Suffolk IP16 4UR
☎ (0728) 642139
Contact: Diana Horner

A diorama of electricity generation. The science and sense of nuclear power and how it works. Electricity from source to our homes and industry. Videos, environmental displays, viewing tower.
Admission: No appointment necessary for visits but guided tours (2 hrs) of power station by prior arrangement only. Open every day 10.00-16.00 hrs. Closed Sun Oct-Mar. Suitable for individuals, groups and school parties. Free.
Directions: 25 miles north of Ipswich. Turn off A12 at Yoxford (B1122) then take Lovers Lane to Sizewell. Nearest railway and bus stations: Saxmundham (8 miles).

See advertisement page 11.

🚗 (50) CP D V

Sudbury

Bulmer Brick & Tile Company Limited

The Brickfields, Bulmer, Sudbury, Suffolk CO10 7EF
☎ (0787) 29232
Contact: Mr P Minter, Managing Director

A family business for over 50 years, the Company makes bricks and specials for the restoration of listed buildings (National Trust, English Heritage, etc). Visitors can see bricks being made in the traditional way. Organised tours (1½ hrs).
Admission: By appointment only. Open Apr-Oct. Mon-Fri 09.00-17.30 hrs. Suitable for groups and school parties of 10-30 people. Age 8+. Group rate £25. Hand-made bricks and plaques made to order.
Directions: From Sudbury to Chelmsford Road take B1058 Sudbury to Castle Hedingham Road. The Brickfields are 1 mile from junct with A131. Nearest railway and bus stations: Sudbury (3 miles).

🚗 CP

Woodbridge

Easton Farm Park

Easton, Wickham Market, Woodbridge, Suffolk IP13 0EQ
☎ (0728) 746475
Contact: Ms C Barbour, Manager

A Victorian farm setting for a working farm with dairy centre, farm animals, vintage machinery, 'stables' tearoom and shop selling unpasteurised milk and souvenirs. Children's playpit. Award-winning nature trail. Milking can be watched from purpose-built overhead walkways.
Admission: No appointment necessary. Open daily Easter to end-Oct 10.30-18.00 hrs. Last admission 16.00-16.30 hrs. Suitable for individuals, families, groups and school parties. Adults £2.75, OAPs £2.15, children under 3 yrs old free, ages 3-16 £1.60. Special reduced rates for groups of 20+ people.
Directions: From A12 take B1116 to Framlingham then follow signs to Easton Farm Park or Easton. Nearest railway station: Wickham Market (4 miles). Nearest bus station: Saxmundham (10 miles).

🚗 CP D R S

ENGLAND

SURREY

Godalming

Thursley Textile Designs

1 Moushill Lane, Milford, Godalming, Surrey
GU8 5BH
☎ (048 68) 24769
Contact: Ms Z O'Brien, Owner

Shop, gallery and workshop selling hand woven articles, tapestries and designer knitwear. Exhibitions in the gallery and various craft courses take place in the workshop. Weaving on hand looms and tapestry. Guided tours (20-60 mins) depending on requirements. Weaving demonstrations and presentation of slides.
Admission: By appointment only (min notice 2 weeks). Open all year Mon-Sat 10.00-17.30 hrs (excl Public Holidays). Suitable for individuals, families, school parties (age 12+) and groups of up to 20 people. £10-£25 according to tour required. Products on sale and weaving, tapestry and knitting commissions taken.
Directions: M25 junct 10, then A3 to Portsmouth. Milford approx 6 miles south of Guildford on A3. Nearest railway station: Milford (1 mile). Nearest bus station: Guildford (7 miles). Nearest bus stop Milford (1 mile).

D S

Woking

Farm and Country Visits

Hermitage Woods Crescent, St John's,
Woking, Surrey GU21 1UF
☎ (048 67) 5379
Contact: Mrs L Lennie, Director

Guided tours (2 hrs+) around a choice of 35 farms throughout Surrey and Hampshire varied in type and location. The farmer gives an informative yet imaginative explanation of his land and animals and visitors can watch important jobs ranging from seasonal cultivations to daily feeding and care of livestock. Teaching material original to each farm available. Occasional opportunities to buy farm products. T-shirts and sweatshirts with slogans can be ordered.
Admission: By appointment only (min notice 4 weeks). Suitable for groups and school parties of 30-60 people (min age 3 yrs). Open all year (excl Public Holidays) times are flexible. Adults £2 (2 hrs), children £1.75 (2 hrs) or £2.50 (4 hrs).
Directions: All farms are in reasonable reach of main roads. Full directions are supplied upon enquiry.

CP

SUSSEX

Bosham

Bosham Walk Craft Centre

Bosham Lane, Bosham, Chichester,
West Sussex PO18 8HX
☎ (0243) 572475
Contact: Mr & Mrs N Petrovic, Proprietors

Fascinating collection of small units in an old-world setting displaying arts, crafts, books and antiques. Many of the craftsmen can be seen at work and demonstrations vary daily incl sculpture, dolls' house making, jewellery, woodturning, wood carving, blacksmithing, porcelain painting, glass engraving etc.
Admission: No appointment necessary. Open all week 10.00-17.30 hrs. (excl 25-27 Dec and 1st week in Feb). Open to individuals, families, school parties (age 9+) and groups of up to 25 children (no limit for adults). Products are on sale.
Directions: Take A259 coast road to roundabout and White Swan pub (3 miles

west of Chichester, 17 miles east of Portsmouth). Take southern exit and follow road for 1 mile into Bosham village. Nearest railway station: Bosham (1 mile). Nearest bus/coach station: Chichester (3 miles).

(100) CP SB S

Heathfield

Merrydown Wine plc

Horam Manor, Horam, East Sussex TN21 0JA
☎ (043 53) 2254
Contact: Ms H Clarke, Tours Supervisor

Producers of the well-known vintage ciders and others. Founded in 1947 and still an independent company. Tour (1 hr), audio presentation and tasting. Shop.
Admission: Appointment advisable but not essential (except min notice 2-3 weeks for Sat). Open all year. Tours Tue-Fri 10.00, 11.15, 14.00 and 15.15 hrs. Suitable for individuals, families, groups and school parties of up to 50 people. Adults £2, children 75p.
Directions: On A267 between Eastbourne and Tunbridge Wells. Nearest railway station: Polegate (8 miles). Nearest bus station: Eastbourne (14 miles).

(50) CP V S

WARWICKSHIRE

Coventry

Massey-Ferguson Tractors Limited

PO Box 62, Banner Lane, Coventry, Warwickshire CV4 9GF
☎ (0203) 852236
Contact: Mrs V Iveson, Visits Co-ordinator
This largest tractor manufacturer in the western world and the UK's largest tractor exporter has customers in more than 150 countries. Guided tours (2 hrs) of manufacturing facilities. Museum, video.
Admission: By appointment (min notice 1 week). Open all year Mon-Fri (excl factory holidays). Tours start 10.00 and 13.30 hrs. Suitable for individuals, families, school parties (age 7+) and groups of up to 60 people.
Directions: M1 junct 17, M45/A45 and then follow A4023 to Banner Lane. Nearest railway and bus stations: Coventry (6 miles).

CP V R

WEST MIDLANDS

Birmingham

Bass Mitchells & Butlers Ltd

Cape Hill Brewery, PO Box 27, Birmingham, West Midlands B16 0PQ
☎ 021-558 1481
Contact: Ms D Barron, Visitor Reception Mgr

The Midlands operating company of Bass plc have been brewing their traditional ales at Cape Hill Brewery since 1879. See the brewing process from the raw materials through to the finished product. Guided tour preceded by video. Admission price also includes coffee (daytime only), ploughman's platter, sample drinks, giveaway and group photograph. Shop.
Admission: By advance appointment only. Open all year (excl Public Holidays) Mon-Sat 11.30-14.00 hrs and Mon-Thur 19.30-22.00 hrs. Suitable for groups of 20-48 people. £4.50.
Directions: From M5 junct 1, take A457 to factory. Nearest railway station: Smethwick (½ mile). Nearest bus station: Birmingham City Centre (1½ miles).

(26-124) CP V S

Cadbury World

PO Box 12, Bournville Lane, Bournville, Birmingham, West Midlands B30 2LU
☎ 021-433 4334
Contact: Mr J Allen

Purpose-built visitor centre at famous factory site. Exhibition tells story of chocolate from Aztec times and how the name of Cadbury became world famous. Demonstration area shows every stage of a chocolate assortment being made. Shop.
Admission: No appointment necessary except for groups of 20+ people. Open every day (excl Christmas Day) Mon-Sat 10.00-17.30 hrs, Sun 12.00-18.00 hrs. Suitable for individuals, families, groups and school parties. Adults £3.75, children £2.75. Groups 10% discount.
Directions: Exit from M5 motorway at junct 2 (southbound) or junct 4 (northbound). From City follow A38 to Bromsgrove and signs for 'south'. Nearest railway station: Bournville (10 mins walk).
See advertisement inside front cover.

(400) CP D V SB S

ENGLAND

Brierley Hill

Royal Brierley Crystal

North Street, Brierley Hill, West Midlands DY5 3SJ
☎ (0384) 70161
Contact: Mrs J West, Visits Administrator

Family-owned company, established in 1776, hand-making full lead crystal glassware. Holder of Royal Warrant since George V's reign. Tours (1 hr) at 11.00, 12.00 and 13.00 hrs showing glassmaking and cutting, craft studio, video and museum. Shop.
Admission: No appointment necessary for individuals and families but appointment required for groups of 6-60 people. Open all year (excl Christmas, Easter week, Spring Bank Holiday week, last week Jul, 1st week Aug, 3rd week Sept). Shop open Mon-Fri 09.30-17.30 hrs, Sat 09.00-17.00 hrs, Sun 10.00-16.30 hrs. Suitable for individuals, school parties (age 7+) and groups. Free.
Directions: From M5 junct 2, take A4123 to Dudley/Wolverhampton. Then A461 to Dudley and Brierley Hill. Nearest railway station: Lye (2 miles). Nearest bus station: Stourbridge (2 miles).

🚗 (100) CP V R S

Solihull

Powergen plc

Haslucks Green Road, Shirley, Solihull, West Midlands B90 4PD
☎ 021-701 2000
Contact: Public Relations Department

See and learn how electricity is generated. A visit takes about 2 hours and includes an introductory talk, followed by a visit to the coal plant, the turbine floor and the control room, led by a station guide.
Admission: Appointment required. Groups are welcome all year Mon-Fri morning, afternoon and evening. Suitable for school parties (age 12+) and groups of 10-24 people. Usually free but check when making booking.
Directions: Contact individual power station for local directions.
See advertisement on page 12.

Walsall

Walsall Leather Centre Museum

Wisemore, Walsall, West Midlands WS2 8EQ
☎ (0922) 721153. Contact: M Glasson, Curator

Working museum based in the capital of the leather goods trade. Visitors can see local leather workers at their trade in authentic workshops. Demonstrations by leather workers explaining their craft. Tours (1 hr) by appointment. Videos of traditional leather crafts.
Admission: No appointment necessary except for guided tours. Open all year Tue-Sat 10.00-17.00 hrs, Sun 12.00-17.00 hrs (Nov-Mar closes every day at 16.00 hrs). Suitable for individuals, families, school parties and groups of up to 40 people. Free. Shop sells range of leather goods. Commissions/orders accepted.
Directions: Off A4148 (ring road). Take Littleton Street exit. Nearest railway and bus stations: Walsall (½ mile).
See advertisement on page 59.

🚗 CP D V SB S

WILTSHIRE

Swindon

South Leaze Sheep Farm

No 1, South Leaze Farm, Swindon, Wiltshire SN1 4NT
☎ (0793) 523134 Contact: Mr S Bell, Owner

Visitors can see ewes lambing in Mar, June, Sept, shearing every weekend in May and June and ewe and lamb feeding all year. Sheep milking and spinning demonstrations, pets corner, visual displays. Picnic and play area. Shop selling products and gifts. Tours (1-2 hrs) on request at 14.30 hrs (earlier for schools).
Admission: No appointment necessary for individuals and families but appointment required (1 week in advance) for groups of up to 60 people. Open 1 Mar-23 Dec Thur-Mon 14.30-17.30 hrs. Suitable for individuals, families, school parties and groups. Adults £1.20, OAPs and children 60p. School parties (up to 100 children) 50p, playgroups 30p.
Directions: M4 exit junct 16 (Great Western Way) to Swindon. Continue for 2 miles then entrance through Queensway & Comet. Nearest railway & bus station: Swindon (1½ miles).

🚗 (30+) CP D S

YORKSHIRE

Hebden Bridge

Maude Walkley Clogs

Canal Wharf Sawmills, Burnley Road,
Hebden Bridge, West Yorkshire HX7 8NH
☎ (0422) 842061
Contact: Mr M Clyndes, Managing Director

Working clog factory dating back to 19th century. Today home to many other traditional crafts, bee museum, art gallery and the unique Enchanted Wood. See the whole clog-making process from sole-cutting to finished product in factory shop. Tour (2 hrs) incl demonstrations/video.
Admission: No appointment necessary. Open all year (excl Christmas Day) Mon-Fri 09.00-17.00 hrs, weekends 09.00-17.30 hrs. Evenings by arrangement. Suitable for individuals, school parties (all ages) and groups. Free. Products for sale incl mail order.
Directions: From M62 take junct 24 for Halifax and then follow signs for Hebden Bridge. Factory on A646 Todmorden-Halifax Rd. Nearest railway station: Hebden Bdge (½ mile).

🚗 (300) D S

Hornsea

Hornsea Pottery

Rolston Road, Hornsea, East Yorkshire
HU18 1UD
☎ (0964) 534211. Contact: Mr K Sellwood, Leisure Amenities Manager

28-acre retail and leisure park surrounding the factory where visitors can watch hand-thrown and cast pottery manufacturing plus decoration processes from a viewing balcony. Discount shop and leisure facilities.
Admission: No appointment necessary. Open daily (but factory operatives do not work Sat, Sun or Bank Holidays). From 10.00-15.45 hrs (Nov-Feb), 10.00-16.45 hrs (Mar-Oct). Suitable for individuals, families, school parties and groups. Min group size 24 people. Day pass for leisure amenities £2.99, OAPs £1.99.
Directions: M62 to Beverley, follow signs to Hornsea and then signs for 'The Pottery'. Nearest railway and bus/coach station: Hull (14 miles).

🚗 (1,000+) CP D R SB S

Sheffield

Abbeydale Industrial Hamlet

Abbeydale Road South, Sheffield,
South Yorkshire S7 2QW
☎ (0742) 367731
Contact: Ms J Peatman, Keeper

Authentic, 18th century water-powered scythe works in situ. Visitors can see the crucible steel furnace, hand forges, manager's house and office and workmens' cottage as well as forging, grinding and other trades. Tours (1-1½ hrs). Shop.
Admission: No appointment necessary except for guided tours. Open all year (excl Christmas) Wed-Sat 10.00-17.00 hrs, Sun 11.00-17.00 hrs. hrs. Suitable for individuals, families, groups and school parties. Adults, OAPs, children £1.50, groups of 20+ people 75p. Family ticket £3.
Directions: On A621 Sheffield-Baslow-Bakewell Road, 4 miles (approx) south of City centre. Nearest railway stations: Dore and Totley (¾ mile), Sheffield City Centre (4 miles). Nearest bus/coach station: Sheffield City Centre (4 miles).

🚗 (20+) CP D V SB S

Kelham Island Industrial Museum

off Alma Street, Sheffield,
South Yorkshire S3 8RY
☎ (0742) 722106
Contact: Mr P Smithurst, Principal Keeper

Major museum of Sheffield industry. 12,000hp steam engine and other working engines and machinery. Visitors can see forging, grinding and making of cutlery, surgical instruments. Audio/visual presentations. Talks for educational groups. Shop.
Admission: No appointment necessary (except for talks). Open all year (excl Christmas) Wed-Sat 10.00-17.00 hrs, Sun 11.00-17.00 hrs. Suitable for individuals, families, school parties, and groups. Adults £1.50, OAPs, children and groups of 20+ people 75p. Family ticket £3.
Directions: Off A616 Sheffield-Barnsley road ½ mile west of City centre. Nearest railway/bus station: Sheffield (1 mile).

ENGLAND

ENGLAND

Thirsk

Treske Limited

Station Works, Thirsk, North Yorkshire
YO7 4NY
☎ (0845) 22770
Contact: Mr J Gormley, Managing Director

A beautiful old maltings where, since 1973, 20 craftsmen have built fine English furniture. Impressive range of woods and designs on display in 8 showrooms. Tours (1/2 hr) during which craftsmen can be seen at work from special walkway. Small gifts and turnery on sale. Commissions for furniture accepted.
Admission: No appointment necesary except for groups of 10+ people. Open all year every day 10.00-17.00 hrs. Suitable for individuals, families and groups of up to 20 people.
Directions: On A61 1 mile from Thirsk. Nearest railway station: Thirsk (50 yds). Nearest bus station: Thirsk (1 mile).

🚗 (15) S

Wakefield

Yorkshire Mining Museum

Caphouse Colliery, New Road, Overton, Wakefield, West Yorkshire WF4 4RH
☎ (0934) 848806
Contact: Mr W Ferris, Commercial Manager

Museum on site of 18th century colliery. Visitors can ride the cage 450ft underground for a rare insight into miners' working life past and present. Displays and continuous audio-visual presentation. Shop.
Admission: No appointment necessary for individuals but min notice 24 hrs for groups of people. Open all year daily (excl Christmas/New Year) 10.00-17.00 hrs. Suitable for individuals, families, school parties (ages 5-16) and groups of 15-200 people. Adults £3.95, OAPs £3.35, children £3.25. Reduced prices for groups. Children under 5 not allowed underground but admitted free.
Directions: On A642 halfway between Wakefield and Huddersfield. Nearest railway and bus station: Wakefield (7 miles).

🚗 (400) CP D V R SB S

York

Maxwell Hemmens Precision Steam Models

'The Steam Gallery', Thorganby, York, North Yorkshire YO4 6DA
☎ (0924) 89331
Contact: Mr M Hemmens, Director

Steam replica specialists and manufacturers of one of the largest ranges of high quality working models and bolt-together kits in the world. Models hand-built at the 'Steam Gallery'. Showroom. Tours (30 mins).
Admission: No appointment necesary except for groups of 5+ people. Open all year Mon-Fri 08.00-17.00 hrs, Sat 08.00-12.30 hrs. Suitable for individuals, families, groups and school parties. Free.
Directions: 6 miles south east of York off A19 Selby to York road. Nearest railway station: York (6 miles).

🚗 (50) CP S

Whisky galore

Only five countries in the world make whisky and, for many drinkers, there is only one that really matters. Curiously enough, the Scots learned how to distill spirits from the monks of what we now know as Ulster, who also brought their bagpipes with them. Their *aqua vitae* translated into the vernacular as *uisge-beathe*, which gave us usque-baugh, usky, wusky and finally whisky.

TRADE SECRETS

Today a great mystique surrounds the making of Scotch whisky — the quality of the burn water from which it is made, the careful selection of maize or barley, the skill of the blender (many blended brands consist of at least twenty different whiskies). But the actual process of distilling is remarkably simple, which is why whisky-making was for centuries a small-scale cottage industry, largely to satisfy domestic demand.

GRAIN OR MALT?

Two kinds of whisky are made in Scotland. Grain whisky is distilled from unmalted barley or maize in the so-called patent or Coffey still, which permits continuous production on an industrial scale. It is only rarely sold unblended. The traditional malt whisky, as the name suggests, is made in a pot still from malted barley that has been dried in peat smoke to give it its distinctive flavour. Most of the whisky sold today is a blend of the two, but the connoisseur's choice — and he has at least two thousand brands from which to make his selection — is unquestionably the single malt, matured in wooden casks for anything up to twenty years or more.

Scotland

Scotland is a country rich in heritage, and a character that's as distinctive as the landscape itself. Many aspects of Scottish life are unique, and the same holds true of its crafts and industries.

Whether it's weaving or glass-making, the salmon farms or the famous whisky distilleries, you'll find the special flavour of Scotland comes out strongly wherever you go. There's a long history of traditional skills here, many of which are to be found nowhere else in Britain. And where the twentieth century has made its mark — as in the impressive hydro-electric schemes in the Scottish Highlands — you'll find a great deal to interest the visitor to this beautiful country.

Much more than Scotch!

They used to say about Glasgow that everything that could be made really was made here, and while things have changed since that Victorian heyday the range of manufacturing and craft industries in Scotland as a whole is as diverse as the country itself.

CHEERS!

Many, of course, are unique. Think of Scotland and whisky immediately springs to mind. In the next few pages you'll find more than a dozen distilleries open to visitors, where you'll enjoy discovering exactly how one of the nation's major exports is produced — and, no doubt, taste a dram or two yourself in the course of your visit.

DISTINCTIVELY SCOTTISH!

But there's much more to the Scots than Scotch. Glassmaking, jewellery and traditional hand-loom weaving are all crafts which have acquired a distinctively Scottish accent north of the Border. Some companies, such as Caithness Glass, have become world-famous for the quality and delicacy of their work. Scotland's textiles industry encompasses both the traditional fabrics such as tweed — to this day often hand-woven in remote cottages in the Highlands and islands — and the weaving of tartan cloths in the mills that have become such a feature of the Border country.

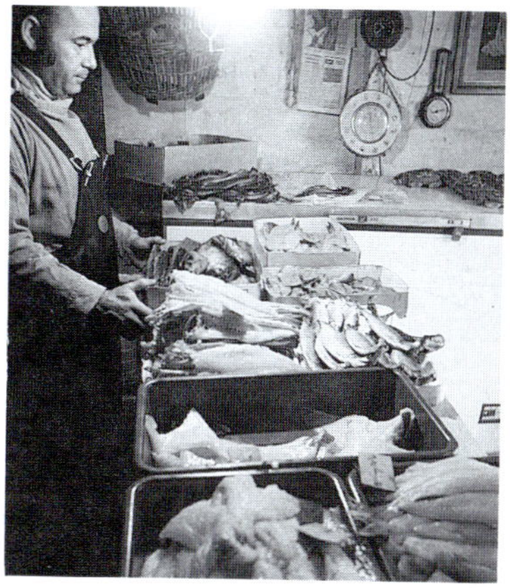

LOCAL DELICACIES

Modern farming methods have ensured that such local delicacies as venison and salmon can now be enjoyed by everyone, and you can see for yourself the care with which these valuable stocks are husbanded. In fact there's almost no end to the variety of Scotland's native industries. In these pages we hope you'll discover much more about the country, and want to spend a fascinating hour or two amid some of Britain's most spectacular and beautiful scenery seeing how it all works.

ARGYLLSHIRE

Cruachan

Scottish Power

Cruachan Power Station
Cruachan, Argyllshire
☎ (086 62) 673
Contact: Mr I Anderson, Publicity & Administrative Officer
or Public Affairs Department, Scottish Power, Cathcart House, Spean Street, Glasgow, Scotland G44 4BE
☎ 041-637 7177

Cruachan generates electricity from water stored high up a Highland mountain. Visitors can see plant at work deep within the mountain power from the hollow mountain! Also mechanical and electrical engineering maintenance and operational work in progress. Guided tours available or visit the Visitor Centre. Display explains how Cruachan was built and operates. Video.
Admission: Appointment not required but coach parties are advised to telephone in advance. Visitors are advised to arrive early during summer. Open Apr-Oct every day 09.00-16.30 hrs. Suitable for individuals, families, groups and school parties. Adults and OAPs £1.25, children 50p. Shop sells souvenirs.
Directions: Cruachan Power Station is on the banks of Loch Awe on main A85 15 miles from Oban.

CP V SB S

Isle of Islay

Bunnahabhain Distillery

Port Askaig, Isle of Islay, Argyllshire, Scotland
☎ (049 684) 646
Contact: Mr H Proctor, Distillery Manager

Malt whisky distillery producing Bunnahabhain 12-year old Single Islay Malt since 1883. Guided tours (1 hr). Products can be bought during visit.
Admission: By appointment only (min notice 1 day). Open all year (excl weekends and Public Holidays) 10.00-16.00 hrs. Suitable for individuals, families, school parties (age 14+) and groups. Max group size 10 people. Free. Unsuitable for disabled people.
Directions: From Port Ellen/airport, follow A846 for approx 20 miles, turn left at signpost and then continue for 4 miles. From Port Askaig, follow A846 for about ¾ mile, take second right as signposted and Distillery is approx 4 miles.

V

Oban

Oban Glassworks

Lochavullin Industrial Estate, Oban, Argyllshire, Scotland PA34 4PL
☎ (0631) 63386
Contact: Ms M Macleod, Factory Shop Manager

See at close quarters the skills of the paperweight maker from shaping molten glass to the finished product. Self-conducted tour (30 mins) to watch production process.
Admission: No appointment required. Open all year Mon-Fri 09.00-17.00 hrs plus Sat Easter-Nov 09.00-13.00 hrs. Suitable for individuals, families, school parties and groups. Free. Products can be bought.
Directions: Follow signs from the town centre. Nearest railway and bus station: Oban (1 mile).

(40+) CP V S

AYRSHIRE

Kilmarnock

John Walker & Son

Hill Street, Kilmarnock, Ayrshire,
Scotland KA3 1HD
☎ (0563) 23401
Contact: Mr W A G Burnet, Reception Mgr

Established in 1820, Johnnie Walker is the largest seller of Scotch whisky in the world today. Visitors see blending and bottling of Scotch whisky. Guided tours (2 hrs). Film or video about Scotch whisky industry given prior to tour of plant.
Admission: Appointment not necessary except for large parties where notice should be given as far in advance as possible (especially during summer months). Open all year (except Public and Local Holidays). Mon-Thur 09.45 and 13.45 hrs, Fri 09.45 hrs. Last admission time 11.45 hrs (or 15.45 hrs for restricted tour). Free. Suitable for individuals, families, school parties and groups. Min age 14. Max group size 100 people. Products for sale.
Directions: Just off A77, 22 miles south of Glasgow. Plant is in town centre immediately north of railway station. Nearest railway station: Kilmarnock (200 yds). Nearest bus station: Kilmarnock (¼ mile).

CP V S

BANFFSHIRE

Dufftown

William Grant & Sons Limited

The Glenfiddich Distillery, Dufftown,
Banffshire, Scotland AB5 4DH
☎ (0340) 20373
Contact: Mrs E A Lafferty,
Scottish Public Relations Manager

Distillers of Glenfiddich Pure Malt Scotch Whisky which first ran from the stills on Christmas Day 1887. Still owned and managed by the Grant family. Glenfiddich is also unique in that it is the only Highland Malt to be bottled on the premises. Audio visual presentation in 6 languages. Guided tour of production, maturation and bottling plus complimentary dram. Guided tours (1½ hrs) 09.30-16.30 hrs.

Please check opening times and admission fees (if any) in advance wherever possible.

Admission: No appointment necessary for individuals and families but appointment necessary for parties of 12+ people (give as much notice as possible especially Jul-Aug). Open all year (excl Christmas/New Year) Mon-Fri 09.30-16.30 hrs and from Easter to mid-Oct on Sat 09.30-16.30 hrs, Sun 12.00-16.30 hrs. Suitable for individuals, families, school parties and groups up to 53 people. Distillery visit free. Products for sale.
Directions: On A941 ½ mile north of Dufftown on north side of Balvenie Castle. Nearest railway station: Keith (10 miles). Nearest bus station: Dufftown (½ mile).

CP D V S

CAITHNESS

Thurso

Dounreay

AEA Technology Dounreay, Thurso,
Caithness, Scotland KW14 7TZ
☎ (0847) 62121 Ext 7255
Contact: Ms C Foreman, Exhibition Manager

Centre for fast reactor research and development work since 1955. The exhibition centre covers all aspects of the nuclear industry. Conducted tours (1 hr+) of fast reactor. Guides available to answer questions. Tours 11.45-14.30 hrs. Assemble 15 mins before start of tour. Shop.
Admission: Open daily Easter to end-Sept 09.00-16.30 hrs. Suitable for individuals, families, school parties and groups of up to 12 people. Free.
Directions: On A836 10 miles west of Thurso. Nearest railway and bus stations: Thurso (10 miles).

(60) CP V SB S

Wick

Caithness Glass plc

Harrowhill, Wick, Caithness, Scotland
KW1 5BP
☎ (0955) 2286
Contact: Ms C Florence, Visitor Services Manager

See glass-blowing at close quarters. Marvel at the skills of the glassmaker from molten glass to the finished product. Self-conducted tour (1 hr).
Admission: No appointment necessary. Open all year Mon-Fri 09.00-17.00 hrs, Sat 09.00-13.00 hrs (May-Sept 09.00-16.00 hrs). Tours Mon-Fri only 09.00-16.30 hrs. Suitable for individuals, school parties, groups. Shop.
Directions: Watch for signs on A9. Situated near the centre of Wick. Nearest railway and bus station: Wick (1 mile).

(50+) CP V S

INVERNESS-SHIRE

Inverness

Culloden Pottery

The Old Smiddy, Gollanfield, Nr Inverness, Inverness-shire, Scotland IV1 2QT
☎ (0667) 62340
Contact: Mr R Park, Partner

Studio pottery hand-made on the premises. Visitors can make their own pot. Special facilities for wheelchair users to 'have a go'. Guided tours (30 mins) by appointment.
Admission: No appointment necesary except for school parties and groups when min notice 7 days required. Open all year (except Christmas/New Year) every day 09.30-17.30 hrs (later in Jul-Sept). Free (£4.40 if making a pot). Extensive gift shop and licensed wholefood vegetarian restaurant.
Directions: Midway between Inverness and Nairn on A96 at Gollanfield crossroads. Nearest railway station and coach station: Nairn (6 miles), Inverness (10 miles).

CP D R SB S

Please mention this guide when making a booking.

Highland Wineries

Moniack Castle, Kirkhill, Inverness, Inverness-shire, Scotland IV5 7PQ
☎ (046 383) 283
Contact: Mr P Guthrie, Production Manager

Producer of quality country wines, liqueurs and preserves. Production began in 1980, based in the 16th century Moniack Castle, using traditional methods. Visitors see the production of wines and preserves in all its stages. Optional guided tour (½ hr). Products can be bought or ordered and delivered.
Admission: No appointment necessary. Open all year (excl Sun) 10.00-17.00 hrs. Suitable for individuals, families and groups of up to 50 people. Unaccompanied children age 16+. Free
Directions: From Inverness, take A862 towards Beauly. ½ mile after Inchmore turn left as signposted. Nearest railway and bus/coach station: Inverness (7 miles).

(20) CP V R SB S

Kingussie

Highland China Limited

Old Station Yard, Kingussie, Inverness-shire, Scotland PH21 1HP
☎ (0540) 661576
Contact: Ms R McIntosh, Administrator

One of Scotland's oldest working potteries in the centre of the Highlands. See all aspects of handcrafted pottery production. Tour (20 mins). Shop selling Highland China pottery.
Admission: No appointment necessary. Open all year daily 08.00-17.00 hrs. Last admission 17.00 hrs. Suitable for individuals, families, groups and school parties. Free.
Directions: On main A9 Perth to Inverness road. Nearest railway station: Kingussie (50 yds). Nearest bus station: Kingussie (200 yds).

(200) CP D V SB S

LANARKSHIRE

Coatbridge

Summerlee Heritage Trust

West Canal Street, Coatbridge, Lanarkshire, Scotland ML5 1QD
☎ (0236) 31261
Contact: Ms S Wingrove, Development Officer

Scotland's noisiest museum brings the past to life. Lively displays of traditional Scottish industries and daily life. Exciting special events, activities and exhibitions. Historic working machinery, regular 'Steam Days'. Daily tram rides. Various demonstrations. Shop.
Admission: No appointment necessary. Open every day (excl Christmas/New Year) 10.00-17.00 hrs. Suitable for individuals, families, groups and school parties. Free.
Directions: From M8 (Coatbridge junct), follow signs to town centre. Nearest railway station: Coatbridge Central (200 yds), Coatbridge Sonnyside (500 yds). Also well served by local buses.

(150+) CP D V SB S

MIDLOTHIAN

Edinburgh

Coloroll Edinburgh Crystal

Eastfield Industrial Estate, Penicuik, Midlothian, Scotland EH26 8HB
☎ (0968) 75128
Contact: Ms M Vincenti, Visitor Centre Mgr

Manufacturers of high-quality lead crystal since 18th century, producing a fine range of hand-crafted glassware. Guided tour (1 hr) demonstrating glass-blowing, cutting and engraving and audio-visual presentation of manufacturing process.
Admission: No appointment necessary. Open all year (excl festive holidays), 09.00-17.00 hrs Mon-Sat (shop), 11.00-17.00 hrs Sun. Last tour 15.30 hrs. Suitable for individuals, families, school parties and groups of up to 100. Children age 10+. Adults £1, children, OAPs and group of 25+ people.
Directions: Leave Edinburgh on the A701 towards Peebles. Travel for approx 10 miles then you will see Edinburgh Crystal signposted on the right. Nearest railway station and bus station: Edinburgh (10 miles).

(60) CP D V R S

SCOTLAND

Scotch Whisky Heritage Centre

358 Castlehill, The Royal Mile, Edinburgh, Midlothian EH1 2NE
☎ 031-220 10441
Contact: Mr G P Melville, Manager

Perfect introduction to the story of whisky brought to life as you travel inside a whisky barrel! Compulsory tours (45 mins) and commentaries available in various languages. Audio visual of whisky making. Shop sells extensive range of scotch whiskies and attractive gifts. Mail order service (UK only).
Admission: No appointment necessary but groups advised to book in advance. Open daily all year (excl Christmas/New Year) 10.00-17.00 hrs (09.00-18.30 hrs in summer). Suitable for individuals, school parties (age 5+) and groups of up to 35 people. Adults £2.50, OAPs £1.50, children £1.25 (ages 5-16). 10% discount for groups of 20+ people.
Directions: Next to Edinburgh Castle in Edinburgh's Royal Mile. Nearest railway station: Waverley (10 mins walk). Nearest bus station: St Andrew's Square (15 mins walk).

D V S

Newtongrange

Scottish Mining Museum

Lady Victoria Colliery, Newtongrange, Midlothian, Scotland EH22 4QN
☎ 031-663 7519
Contact: Ms C McLeod, Receptionist

Scotland's national museum of the coal industry. On 2 sites— Lady Victoria Colliery and Prestongrange of particular interest to educational groups. Exhibition, talking tableaux, colliery tours and working winding engine. Guided tour (1 hr) every ½ hr. Videos available for booked parties. Shop.
Admission: No appointment necessary. Open all year Tue-Fri 10.00-16.30 hrs, weekends 12.00-17.00 hrs. Suitable for individuals, school parties and groups of up to 60 people. Adults £1.25, OAPs & children 80p.
Directions: Lady Victoria Colliery is south of Edinburgh at Newtongrange. Nearest railway station: Edinburgh (9 miles). Nearest bus station: Dalkeith (2 miles). Prestongrange is on B1348 south of Musselburgh at Prestonpans. Nearest railway station: Prestonpans. Nearest bus station: Joppa.

🚗 (72) CP V R S

MORAYSHIRE

Elgin

James Johnston & Co of Elgin Limited

The Mill Shop & Cashmere Visitor Centre, Newmill, Elgin, Morayshire, Scotland IV30 2AF
☎ (0343) 549319
Contact: Ms W Proctor, Retail Manager

Old-established manufacturers of high-quality cashmere and fine wool fabrics and knitwear. Audio visual presentation in 6 languages. Mill tours (45 mins) by appointment to see production of cashmeres and fine woollens from raw raw material to finished textiles. Products can be bought.
Admission: No appointment necessary for individuals and families. Cashmere visitor centre open all year Mon-Sat 09.00-17.30 hrs, 09.00-19.30 hrs Jul to end-Sept. Groups and tours by appointment Mon-Thur 11.00 or 14.00 hrs.
Directions: A96 Aberdeen-Inverness. Enter Pansport Road, continuing across River Lossie to Newmill Road. Nearest railway station and bus/coach station: Elgin (¾ mile).

🚗 CP D V SB S

SCOTLAND

PERTHSHIRE

Bankfoot

Porridge Press Printers

The Auld Police Hoose, 'Strathcluanie',
Dunkeld Road, Bankfoot, Perthshire,
Scotland PH1 4AJ
☎ (0738) 87225
Contact: Mrs S Davidson, Proprietor

Letterpress printers producing a wide range of goods in tiny workshop. Unusual hand-crafted greetings cards. Items and displays of historical interest. Demonstrations of letterpress printing by arrangement. Shop. **Admission:** No appointment necessary for individuals but advisable. School parties by appointment only. Open all year Mon-Fri usually 10.00-16.00 hrs (or by appointment). Suitable for individuals, families and groups of up to 6 people. Free. No smoking. No dogs. **Directions:** Off A9 8 miles north of Perth, 18 miles south of Pitlochry just south of Birnam/Dunkeld. Take B867 loop road to Bankfoot and situated north end of village. Nearest railway and bus station: Dunkeld (4 miles), Perth (8 miles).

🚗 S

Blair Atholl

John Ridley Projects Limited

The Mill, Blair Atholl, Perthshire,
Scotland PH18 5SH
☎ (079 681) 321
Contact: Mr S Page, Mill Manager

Working water mill established in 1613 producing stoneground flour and oatmeal by traditional methods. Visitors can also see grain drying, milling oats and wheat, packaging, baking bread, scones etc. Guided tours (30 mins). **Admission:** No appointment necessary. Open 1 Apr-31 Oct Mon-Fri 10.00-17.30 hrs, Sun 12.00-17.30. Last admission 17.00 hrs. Suitable for individuals, families, groups and school parties (age 8+) of up to 20 people. Adults 75p, children 60p. No smoking, no stiletto heels in mill. Products sold in shop. **Directions:** From A9 Perth to Inverness road, take turning to Blair Atholl. Signposted Blair Castle and Corn Mill 1 mile. Nearest railway station: Blair Atholl (50 yds). Nearest bus station: Pitlochry (7 miles).

🚗 (50) CP R S

Crieff

Glenturret Distillery Limited

The Hosh, Crieff, Perthshire, Scotland
PH7 4HA
☎ (0764) 2424
Contact: Mr P J M Fairlie, Managing Director

Scotland's oldest Highland malt distillery. Guided tours (25-30 mins) and free taste of the The Glenturret. Award-winning visitor centre, audio-visual presentation and 3-D exhibition. Whisky tasting bar, Smugglers Restaurant, Pagoda Room and shop. **Admission:** No appointment necessary but notice required for groups. Open Mar-Dec Mon-Sat 09.30-16.30 hrs. Suitable for individuals, families, school parties and groups. Max capacity 200 visitors per hr. Adults £1.75, OAPs £1.40, children ages 12-17 70p. 10% reductions for groups of 40 or more people. **Directions:** On A85 north west of Crieff. Nearest railway station: Perth (16 miles). Nearest bus/coach station: Crieff (½ mile).

🚗 (120) CP V R S

Grange by Errol

Scotherbs

Watery Butts, Grange by Errol, Perthshire,
Scotland PH2 7SZ
☎ (082 12) 228
Contact: Mr S Turner or Mr R Wilson, Partners

Cultivation of an extensive range of culinary herbs in garden and under cover. Demonstration kitchen. Plants and fresh-cut herbs available, also herb-based mustards, oils and vinegar. Tour (1 hr) by arrangement. Cookery and herb garden design classes available. Shop. **Admission:** No appointment necessary. Open daily mid-Apr to mid-Oct 10.30-16.00 hrs, Mon-Fri mid-Oct to mid-Apr 10.30-16.00 hrs. Suitable for individuals, families, school parties (age 15+) and groups of up to 30 people. Free. Details of classes available on application. No dogs. **Directions:** From A85 turn off at Inchture, take Errol road and Scotherbs is 2 miles east of Errol off B958. Nearest railway and bus station: Dundee or Perth (11 miles).

🚗 (30) CP D R S

SCOTLAND

Highland Tryst Museum

The Weavers House, Burrell Street, Crieff, Perthshire, Scotland PH7 4DG
☎ (0764) 5202
Contact: Ms P MacDonald, Curator

Hand-loom tartan weaving involving natural dyeing in 18th century weaver's house. Tartan weaving in wool and silk, hand-spinning, sporran making and leather carving. Guided tours showing artisans working. Video/audio presentations.
Admission: No appointment necessary for individuals but min notice of 1 week for groups of 20+ people, less for smaller groups. Open Apr-Oct every day 09.00-18.30 hrs, Oct-Apr 10.00-16.30 hrs (closed Sun). Last admission 18.30 hrs in summer, 16.30 hrs in winter. Suitable for individuals, families, school parties and groups of up to 50 people. Adults £1.50, OAPs £1, children 50p, family £3. Reduced rates for groups of 20+ people. Products for sale. Orders accepted.
Directions: In Crieff on the A822. Nearest railway station: Perth (17 miles). Nearest bus station: Crieff.

🚗 CP R SB S

Lower City Mills

West Mill Street, Perth, Perthshire, Scotland PH1 5QP
☎ (0738) 30572
Contact: Mr N A Smith, Proprietor

Built in 1787 on the site of Perth's mediaeval town mills, this restored oatmeal mill is powered by Scotland's largest working waterwheel. Visitors can see the production of stoneground organic oatmeal and wholewheat flour. Guided tours (½ hr) any time by prior arrangement for groups.
Admission: No appointment for individuals but min notice 1 week for groups. Open Easter to end-Oct Mon-Sat 10.00-17.30 hrs, Sun 12.00-17.30 hrs. Other times by appointment. Suitable for individuals, families, school parties (age 5+) and groups of 10-50 people. Adults and OAPs £1, children (under 18) 70p. No unaccompanied children. Oatmeal, flour etc to order and on sale.
Directions: Take M90, A9, A85 to Perth. Mill is situated near town centre and is signposted 'Working Watermill' from inner ring road. Nearest railway and bus station: Perth (½ mile).

🚗 (200) CP D V R SB S

Perth

Caithness Glass plc

Inveralmond, Perth, Perthshire, Scotland PH1 3TZ
☎ (0738) 37373
Contact: Mr I Mutch, Retail Manager

See at close quarters the skills of paperweight making from the raw material to the finished product. Visitors will also see lampwork and glassmaking. Self-conducted tour (1 hr) Mon-Fri 09.00-16.30 hrs.
Admission: Open all year excl Christmas/New Year. Last admission time 17.00 hrs. Suitable for individuals, families, groups and school parties. Products for sale in factory shop Mon-Sat 09.00-17.00 hrs, Sun 11.00-17.00 hrs (Jul and Aug open until 18.00 hrs every day). Within technical limitations orders for anything in glass or paperweights considered.
Directions: On main A9 trunk road on Perth western by-pass on the northern edge of town. Nearest railway and bus station: Perth (3 miles).

🚗 (120) CP D V R S

STRATHCLYDE

Dumbarton

Allied Distillers Limited

2 Glasgow Road, Dumbarton, Strathclyde, Scotland G82 1ND
☎ (0389) 65111
Contact: Mr I Burt, Head of Public Relations

At Kilmalid see the modern fully automated operation where the world famous Ballantine's and Teacher's Scotch whiskies are produced. Mature Scotch whisky arrives in oak barrels and is blended then bottled. Guided tours (1 hr max) at 10.00 Mon-Fri, 14.00 hrs Mon-Thur.
Admission: By appointment only (min notice 1 day required by telephone). Open all year (excl July) Mon-Thur 10.00-16.30 hrs, Fri 10.00-13.00 hrs. Closed Sat, Sun. Suitable for individuals, school parties (age 14+) and groups of 8-50 people. Free. Unsuitable for elderly and infirm.
Directions: Take Bonhill turning off A82 roundabout at Dumbarton. Proceed 1 mile to Vale of Leven Industrial Estate. Allied Distillers is the first site. Nearest railway station: Dumbarton Central (2 miles).

🚗 (100) CP V

WESTERN ISLES

South Uist

Hebridean Jewellery

Iochdar, South Uist, Western Isles, Scotland PA81 5QX
☎ (087 04) 288
Contact: Mr J Hart, Proprietor

Manufacturer of silver and gold jewellery. Established in 1974 in a small croft outhouse but moved into purpose-built premises in 1981. Designs and makes to customers' specifications. Shop, mail order and supplies worldwide. Visitors see gas soldering, filing, sawing, fabricating and polishing.
Admission: Open all year Mon-Sat 09.00-15.00 hrs. Suitable for individuals, families, school parties and groups of up to 40 people. Free. Shop.
Directions: Situated on north-western shore of South Uist about 2 miles west of the A865 in Iochdar (50 yds past telephone box). Turn right and factory visible 300 yds away.

🚗 (6) CP D S

SCOTLAND

Breathing life into glass

Some of the finest glassmakers in the world are to be found in Britain. Every manufacturer has his own traditions, his own special techniques, his own well-kept secrets. But however they may differ in detail, the processes they use have much in common, and have changed little over the past few centuries since glass was first made on an industrial scale.

OUT OF THE FURNACE

Glass is essentially an amalgam of sand, soda and lime. The basic ingredients used to make lead crystal are silica, lead oxide and potassium carbonate, with other chemicals added to enhance the purity or create colour effects. The lead is responsible for the considerable weight of the finished crystalware. These raw materials — selected and prepared with great care — are heated for up to 36 hours inside a furnace while they fuse together at controlled temperatures of around 1200°C.

The molten 'metal' is then ready for blowing, a job calling for precise and finely honed skills. From the furnace the flower scoops up or 'gathers' a quantity of glass on the end of a hollow blowing-iron, several feet long. This is then smoothed and roughly formed against a curved block to the approximate shape required. The worker then literally blows through the rod to create the hollow cavity, just like inflating a large, heavy and extremely hot balloon. He has to work deftly, because the molten glass soon begins to set, and sometimes whole teams of gatherers and blowers work together on the same piece. The blowing action has to be carefully controlled, for on it depends not just the initial shaping — the full shape is usually achieved by then blowing the glass in a mould — but the all-important thickness of the glass. If the glass cools too quickly stresses may be set up in its structure, and so it is annealed by a process that lets it reach normal temperatures at a much reduced rate, usually by moving it extremely slowly along a conveyor belt in a cooling chamber.

CUTTING AND ENGRAVING

When cool the near-invisible outline of blown glass is ready for cutting. The blank shape is marked in ink with a grid of lines which indicate the pattern to be cut. From this point on, the cutter works largely from memory as, using stone cutting wheels with flat or wedge-shaped edges, he makes a complex and precise series of incisions to the required depth. It is slow and painstaking work, calling for patience and a steady hand. Even a small item may require several hours' work from the cutter; on the larger presentation pieces, a whole team of cutters may be at work for days at a time. Special pieces of glassware may also feature an engraved design. This is first drawn freehand on the surface before being etched into the glass using small copper cutting wheels. As with every aspect of the production process, everything depends on the skill of the craftsmen involved at each stage. For this reason no two pieces of traditionally made glassware or crystal are ever quite the same. Each is a unique statement of the glassmaker's art, born in the shimmering heat of the furnace, shaped with the living breath of the blower, decorated by hand until it is a glittering masterpiece, the perfect fusion of art and technology.

Wales

Wales paid a critical role in shaping the Industrial Revolution. Coal, iron, copper and slate were won from her hills and valleys, dramatically transforming the landscape. Now that those industries have contracted, we are once more aware of the wild grandeur of the Rhondda or the great slate mountains of Snowdonia, and of how they must have looked generations ago.

But the traditional industries have not entirely vanished from Wales. They have been joined in recent times both by the hi-tech and by a steady expansion of many much older skills — the potters, weavers, jewellers and craftsmen who have come to these quiet folds to practise their individual arts, ensuring their survival for decades to come.

To visit Wales is not just to be in some of the most beautiful landscapes in the world. It is to see past infusing present, and vice versa, in a way rarely found elsewhere .

The traditional and the new

A century ago the natural wealth of Wales — its coal and iron ore, its copper and slate — was critical to Britain's industrial prosperity. The valleys were lined by pitheads and the long, snaking terraces of miners' cottages. In the north, colossal cliffs of slate towered above the houses, and quarries the size of volcanic craters steadily inched their way into the mountains to feed the endless appetite for slates in the growing industrial towns. The famous narrow-gauge railways of Wales — the Festiniog and the Talyllyn, for instance — are now tourist attractions of international importance, yet practically every one of them was built simply to transport the endless wagon-loads of slates from quarry to quarry.

THE VALLEYS AND THE MOUNTAIN

Along the famous Heads of the valleys road you can see where huge blast furnaces turned night into day, until Merthyr Tydfil became the greatest centre of iron production in the world.

The first steam locomotive in the world was built near here, a quarter of a century before the *Rocket*. Over the year thousands flocked to see the great copper mine at Parys Mountain on Anglesey — a sight judged by many to be the equal of the might castle at Conwy — while in the rural areas and small towns the looks of the textile industry were a major challenge to the dominance of the great mills of Lancashire and Yorkshire.

LOCAL PRIDE

There is still tremendous pride in Wales and its industries, and there is much for the casual observer to see. Several centres have been established where visitors can be shown at first hand their typical working practices, and a selection is listed on these pages.

DYFED

Nevern

Nevern Dairies Limited

Nevern, Nr Newport, Dyfed, West Wales
SA42 0NQ
☎ (0293) 820354
Contact: Mr A Threipland, Director, Dairy Office

Opened in December 1986, the Dairy makes both traditional and block Cheddar, Caerphilly and other cheeses producing about 30 tonnes of cheese per week. Visitors see the production of cheese from milk to final product and storage of cheese on open shelves. Visit takes about 20-30 mins.
Admission: No appointment necessary. Open all year daily 09.30-16.30 hrs, Last admission 16.15 hrs. Free. Suitable for individuals, groups and school parties up to 20 people. Max capacity of 25 visitors. Products for sale. Orders taken for all products including all sizes of cheese, butter etc.
Directions: Leaving Cardigan on the A40 towards Fishguard, travel for about 3 miles until you reach the village of Croft, turn right and follow signs. Nearest railway station: Fishguard (10 miles). Nearest bus station: Newport (3 miles).

🚗 (50) CP S

Pembroke

Pembroke Power Station

West Pennar, Pembroke, Dyfed, South Wales
SA71 5SS
☎ (0646) 641321
Contact: Mr P A Randall, Station Administration Officer

Large oil-fired power station generating 2000mw in airy, modern buildings set in green, landscaped valley. Organised tours (1 hr) June-Sept Tue, Wed and Thur at 14.00 and 15.00 hrs.
Admission: By appointment only Oct-May (min notice 1 week). Suitable for individuals, families and school parties and groups of 5-30 people. Free. Min age 10+. No pets.
Directions: A477 Carmarthen to Pembroke, then B4319/4320 to West Pennar. Nearest railway and coach station: Pembroke (7 miles).

🚗 (25) CP D V

GWENT

Magor

The Whitbread Beer Company

The Brewery, Magor, Gwent, Wales NP6 3DA
☎ (0633) 880661
Contact: Mrs R Davies, Public Relations Asst.

This impressive modern brewery annually brews more than 1½ millon barrels of Heineken, Stella Artois, Whitbread Best Bitter and other ales. Visitors tour the main brewery departments and the bustling canning and kegging halls. Organised tour (1½ hrs). Video. Promotional items on sale.
Admission: Appointment necessary (min notice 3 weeks). Open most of year Tue-Thur 10.00-14.30 hrs. Suitable for groups and school parties of 10-30 people. Adults and children £3 (but special rate for school parties), OAPs £2.50.
Directions: By junct 23 on M4. Follow signs to Langstone. Nearest railway and bus station: Newport (6 miles).

🚗 (15) CP V S

Please mention this guide when making a booking.

GWYNEDD

Blaenau Ffestiniog

Ffestiniog Pumped-Storage Power Station

Ffestiniog Information Centre, Tan-y-Grisiau,
Blaenau Ffestiniog, Gwynedd,
North Wales LL41 3TP
☎ (0766) 830310
Contact: Mrs B Roberts, Visits Officer

The first pumped-storage power station in the UK which opened in 1963. Water is stored and used to generate electricity. Slide/tape presentation prior to tour (2 hrs) which starts every hour from 10.30-15.30 hrs.
Admission: By appointment (min notice 1 week). Open daily Easter-Oct 10.00-16.30 hrs. Other times by prior arrangement. Last admission 15.30 hrs. Adults £1.25, students/OAPs 80p, children 70p. Free access to Upper Dam for min group size of 7 people. Limited tour available for those unable to climb stairs or walk far. Suitable for individuals, school parties and groups of 7-53 people. Shop.
Directions: Off A496 at Tan-y-Grisiau on the edge of Snowdonia National Park. Nearest railway and bus stations: Blaenau Ffestiniog (1 mile).

(25) CP SB S

Gloddfa Ganol Slate Mine

Blaenau Ffestiniog, Gwynedd, North Wales
LL41 3NB
☎ (0766) 830664
Contact: Mr W E Roberts, Managing Director

Walk into the enormous underground chambers blasted out of the mountain by miners working the slate cliffs by candlelight. View the open cast blasting operations from the safety of the observation gallery, In the mill visitors can see slate rocks being split into roofing slates, hearths and building stone. Plan your visit of 2-4 hrs between 10.00-17.30 hrs. Also extra guided tours of old mine workings (1 hr). 2 video films, demonstrations.
Admission: No appointment necessary. Open Easter-Sept Mon-Fri 10.00-17.30 hrs. Last admission 16.30 hrs. Suitable for individuals, families, school parties and groups. Adults and OAPs £2.75, children £1.25 (accompanied by adults only). Special reduced

group rates 10% discount (plus extra 10% if paid in advance). Shop. Orders accepted.
Directions: On A470 one mile north of Blaenau Ffestiniog. Nearest railway station: Blaenau Ffestiniog (1 mile). Bus service available from station to site.

(200) CP D V R SB S

Llechwedd Slate Caverns

Blaenau Ffestiniog, Gwynedd, North Wales
LL41 3NB
☎ (0766) 830306
Contact: Mr L P Manley, General Manager

2 exciting underground tours into the heart of a slate mine. Victorian workings and demonstrations of slate splitting, dressing, old drilling techniques etc. Various audio/video presentations below ground and interpretative displays on surface. Tours (½ hr) start at 10.00 hrs.
Admission: Open all year 10.00-17.30 hrs. Last admission 17.15 hrs in summer, 16.15 hrs in winter. For 1 tour adults £3.25, OAPs £2.75, children £2.25. For 2 tours adults £5, OAPs £4, children £3.50. 10% reduction for groups of 20+ people. Suitable for individuals, families, school parties and groups. Products for sale and special commissions for slate products, designs etc undertaken.
Directions: Approach from Betws y Coed/ Llandudno A470, or Porthmadoc on A487. Nearest railway and bus station: Blaenau Ffestiniog (½ mile).

(300) CP D V R SB S

WALES

Nuclear Electric

Trawsfynydd Power Station, Trawsfynydd, Blaenau Ffestiniog, Gwynedd, North Wales LL41 LDT
☎ (076 687) 331
Contact: Ms M Williams, Receptionist

The only Magnox nuclear power station built inland using a lake for cooling purposes. Guided tour (2 hrs) includes the Reactor Viewing Gallery, Turbine Hall and Control Room. Introductory audio/visual presentation. Pre-booked tours Mon-Fri 10.30 and 13.30 hrs.
Admission: Appointment required (min notice 4 weeks). Open all year Mon-Fri. Evening and weekend tours by special arrangement only. Suitable for school parties (age 11+) and groups of 6-50 people. Free. Souvenirs available.
Directions: On A470 in Gwynedd between Dolgellau and Ffestiniog north of Trawsfynydd. Nearest railway and bus station: Blaenau Ffestiniog (7 miles).
See advertisement page 11.

🚗 CP D V R S

Caernarfon

Inigo Jones & Company Ltd

Tudor Slateworks, Groeslon, Caernarfon, Gwynedd, North Wales LL54 7ST
☎ (0286) 830242
Contact: Mr J F Lloyd, Director

Established in 1861 to make school writing slates, the Company now specialises in architectural, monumental and slatecraft work. Visitors can see slate cutting and polishing machinery in use and hand and machine letter cutting. Video. Audio commentaries in workshop. Shop.
Admission: No appointment necessary except for large parties when 24 hrs notice required. Open all year. Easter-Sep Mon-Fri 09.00-16.30 hrs, weekends 10.00-16.30 hrs. Oct-Easter Mon-Fri 09.00-16.30 hrs, weekends 09.00-12.00 hrs. Suitable for individuals, families, school parties (ages 6-18) and groups. Adults £1.50, OAPs and children £1.00. Groups of 20-50 people 20% discount.
Directions: On A487 Caernarfon-Porthmadog Rd between Groeslon & Penygroes. Nearest railway station: Bangor (12 miles). Nearest bus station: Caernarfon (5 miles).

🚗 (50) CP D V SB S

WALES

Cemaes Bay

Nuclear Electric

Wylfa Power Station and Information Centre Cemaes Bay, Isle of Anglesey, Gwynedd, North Wales LL67 0DH
☎ (0407) 710471
Contact: Ms H Walton, Sect Head, Services

The largest and most advanced Magnox nuclear power station in the world producing 840 megawatts of electricity. Introductory talk and video. Guided tour (approx 2½ hrs). Information centre with exhibition. Cinema.
Admission: No appointment necessary for individuals or families but appointment required for school parties (age 11+) and groups (min notice 4 weeks). Information centre open all year Mon-Fri and Bank Holiday weekends. 10.00-16.30 hrs. Closed 25 & 26 Dec and New Year's Day. Guided tours of power station at 10.30 and 14.00 hrs. Evening tours by arrangement only. Free. Suitable for groups of 6-50 people. Souvenirs available from Information Centre.
Directions: On A5025 between Holyhead and Cemaes Bay, Anglesey. Information Centre is off Power Station access road. Nearest railway station: Holyhead (15 miles).
See advertisement page 11.

🚗 CP V S

Llanberis

Dinorwig Pumped Storage Power Station

Dinorwig Information Centre,
Museum of the North, Llanberis, Gwynedd,
North Wales LL55 4UR
☎ (0286) 870936
Contact: Mrs J Parry, Visits Officer

A power station built inside a mountain on the edge of Snowdonia National Park. Water stored and used to generate electricity. Tour (2 hrs) and multi-media presentation. Journey underground to power station. Shop.
Admission: No appointment necessary. Open all year daily (except Christmas) 10.00-17.00 hrs. Suitable for individuals, families, groups and school parties (age 5+). Max group size 50 people.
Directions: Take A5 to Bangor, turn left at Capel Curig (A4086) After 4 miles turn right towards Llanberis. Nearest railway station: Bangor (7 miles). Nearest bus station: Llanberis (¼ mile).

🚗 (80) CP D V SB S

POWYS

Llanwrtyd Wells

The Cambrian Factory

Llanwrtyd Wells, Powys, Wales LD5 4SD
☎ (059 13) 211
Contact: Mr M Pott, General Manager

Designers and manufacturers of Welsh wool, tweeds and fashionwear for men and women. Mill factory dating from 1900. Visitors can see spinning and weaving from fleece to finished cloth. Shop.
Admission: No appointment necessary. Open all year (excl Public Holidays) Mon-Fri 08.15-16.30 hrs. Shop open until 17.15 hrs and all day Sat in summer. Free. Suitable for individuals, families, groups and school parties of up to 30 people.
Directions: From M4, take A4042 to Abergavenny then A40 through Crickhowell to intersection. Take A479/A470 to Builth, then A483. Nearest railway and bus station: Llanwrtyd Wells (1½ miles).

🚗 (30) CP D SB S

WALES

Power to the people

Britain has an insatiable appetite for electricity — for the home, for the office, for industry. So great is the demand, in fact, that supplying that need has created what is in its own right one of the largest industries in the country.

FIRST PRINCIPLES

Electricity can be produced in several ways. If you turn a loop of wire within the field of a magnet, a small electrical curent will be produced. This is, in essence, the principle adopted on an infinitely larger scale in our power stations, except that the magnet revolves

within the loop. Several sources of energy are used — coal, oil, nuclear fusion, hydro-electric power. Tremendous force is needed to turn the shaft of the generator against the resistance of the magnetic field but this energy is converted to electrical current in the coils.

THE POWER STATION AT WORK

At a typical large coal-fired power station coal arrives round the clock in thousand-ton 'merry-go-round' trains which discharge their load while still on the move. According to need it will either by stockpiled or conveyed direct to the boiler house. Here the coal is pulverised as fine as talcum powder before being fed into the boilers and burned. The heat thus produced

turns water circulating in the tubes lining the boiler into high-pressure steam. This in turn drives a steam turbine connected to the main generator. The spent steam is then condensed back into water by passing it over cooling tubes or vanes which have their own circuit of cold water taken from a nearby river or, in some cases, the sea. The cooling towers create a draught which passes through the warm cooling water as it is sprinkled down inside them as part of the recycling process. This creates clouds of water vapour which can sometimes be seen coming from the tops of the towers.

HYDRO-ELECTRIC POWER

In mountainous parts of the country — such as in North Wales or the Scottish Highlands — a number of hydro-electric power stations have been built to take advantage of natural resources. Rainfall is gathered in dams ready to be released so that it will flow through the turbines in the power station below, just as if it were driving a waterwheel. The power generated depends on the volume of water passing through and also the height — or 'head' — from which it is piped. A hydro-electric power station can thus be started up very quickly once the dam is opened, which can be very useful if there is a sudden high demand. In summer, when water supplies are necessarily limited, Britain's hydro-electric power stations are largely used to supplement the output of stations relying on other energy sources. They are employed most efficiently in winter, when heavier consumer demand for electricity is matched by the power stations' ability to supply it through the larger volume of water stored and constantly replenished in the dams during the winter rains.

Northern Ireland

The heritage of Northern Ireland is still largely rural, and it is very much an outdoor country. Driving along those quiet roads, you can from time to time catch echoes of more distant times: ploughing with heavy horses, turf-cutting, scything and thatching.

The ancient kings of Ulster, they say, liked their harps strung with gold but today's craftsmen — for they still make harps the traditional way in Northern Ireland — will tell you that bronze is best. Such skills are often handed down from generation to generation, and in these pages you can find details of some of the many fascinating trades and crafts that are carried on all over the country, and which are only too delighted to open their doors to visitors.

A treasure of crafts & industries

Everyone likes to bring something away with them from their holiday and in Northern Ireland you'll find many places where you can see things being made before you buy them — a fascinating way to shop.

TWO OF THE BEST!

Two of its most celebrated industries are Ireland's famous whiskey, and the equally distinctive pure Irish linen for so long associated with Belfast. The Irish origins of whiskey (with an 'e') are lost among the mists of time, though as early as 1276 there are records of 'a mighty draught' being given to soldiers by the landlord of Bushmills, where today there is the oldest licensed distillery in the world, dating back to 1608. Sir Walter Raleigh had a 32-gallon cask of 'uisce bheatha' (water of life) with him on the voyage to America and Peter the Great, no less, preferred 'Irish' to all else.

THE 'ENGINE ROOM'

Belfast has traditionally been Ulster's engine room. During the Industrial Revolution the development of industries like linen, rope-making, shipbuilding (Belfast was the birthplace of the *Titanic*, and the world's largest dry dock is here) and tobacco caused it to double in size every ten years. When Arthur Young visited Ulster in the 1770s he was astonished by the size and extent of the linen industry; he saw 'a whole province peopled by weavers' and there is still much to be seen of the industry's place in Ireland, both past and present.

Today, in fact, Ulster's range of crafts and industries is an exceptional one — cut-glass goblets, decanters and bowls; creamy Belleek pottery; pure wool jumpers and cardigans hand-knitted in traditional patterns; hand-embroidered wall-hangings; hand-made quilting; Carrickmacross lace and polished Mourne granite. Treasure it for what it is - the work of individual craftsmen and women, some of the finest to be found anywhere in Britain.

N. IRELAND

ANTRIM

Bushmills

The 'Old Bushmills' Distillery Company Limited

Bushmills, Co Antrim, Northern Ireland
BT57 8XH
☎ (026 57) 31521
Contact: Tour Department

Distillation, blending, bottling and despatch of Company brands of Irish whiskey all take place at the oldest licensed whiskey distillery in the world. Tours see the complete whiskey making process from mashing to bottling. Guided tours (1 hr) include hospitality time. A visit to shops only can be arranged.
Admission: Telephone call in advance is recommended. Open all year (except 16 Apr, 7 May, 12-13 Jul, 1-5 Oct and 24 Dec 1990-1 Jan 1991) Mon-Thur 09.00-12.00 hrs and 13.30-15.30 hrs, Fri 09.00-11.45 hrs.
Last admission time Mon-Thur 15.30 hrs, Fri 11.45 hrs. Free at present but under review. Suitable for individuals and groups. Parties divided into groups of approx 20 people. Max capacity for visitors approx 500 per day. Coach parties by prior arrangement only. Products for sale.
Directions: In Coleraine, take B17 to village of Bushmills. Follow signs through village to distillery. Nearest railway and bus station: Coleraine (8 miles).
See advertisement on opposite page.

🚗 (50) CP V S

FERMANAGH

Belleek

Belleek Pottery Limited

Belleek, Fermanagh, Northern Ireland
BT93 3FY
☎ (036 565) 501
Contact: Mrs P McCauley, Manageress, Visitor Centre

Ireland's oldest pottery dating from 1857. All pieces are handcrafted in the distinctive cream-coloured porcelain including intricate 'woven' baskets. Visitors can see craftsmen making, glazing and decorating the porcelain. Tours of factory (30 mins) available. Video (20 mins) on the history of the Pottery and the handcrafted process.
Admission: No appointment necessary except for large groups. Tours Mon-Fri 09.30-12.15 hrs and 14.15-16.15 hrs (last tour 15.30 hrs on Fri). Shop open Apr-Oct Mon-Fri 09.00-18.00 hrs, Sat 10.00-18.00 hrs, Sun 14.00-18.00 hrs. Nov-Mar Mon-Fri 09.00-17.50 hrs. Suitable for individuals, families, school parties and groups of up to 25 people. Adults, OAPs and children £1 (children under 12 free). Special reduced group rate 50p for groups of 20+ people. Products for sale.
Directions: Follow A46 from Enniskillen to Belleek. Nearest bus station: Enniskillen (24 miles). Regular bus service to Belleek.
See advertisement on opposite page.

🚗 (100) CP D V R

TYRONE

Dungannon

Tyrone Crystal

Killybrackey, Coalisland Road, Dungannon, Northern Ireland BT71 6TT
☎ (086 87) 26688
Contact: Sales Department

Formed in 1970, the Company produces mouth-blown, hand-cut full lead crystal stemware, bowls, vases and table accessories. Visitors can see blowing, marking, cutting and polishing of the glassware. Tours of factory (1 hr) are available. Video (15 mins) describes the history of the Company and the production processes.
Admission: No appointment necessary except for large groups where min notice of 1 day required. Open all year (excl Public Holidays). Tours Mon-Thur 09.00-17.00 hrs, Fri 09.00-13.30 hrs. Last tour Mon-Thur 16.00 hrs, Fri 12.00 hrs. Shop open Mon-Fri 09.00-17.00 hrs, Sat 10.00-16.00 hrs. Suitable for individuals, families, school parties and groups of up to 15 people. Free. Orders or commissions accepted.
Directions: From M1 junct 15 take A29 to Dungannon. Nearest bus station: Dungannon (1½ miles). Regular bus service.
See advertisement on opposite page.

🚗 (100) CP D V SB S

N. IRELAND

Northern Ireland Tourist Board

A wealth of tradition and fine craftsmanship in a land of scenic beauty.

For a complete list of workplaces to visit in Northern Ireland contact:

Tourist Information Centre
48 High Street
Belfast BT1 2DS
☎ (0232) 246609 fax (0232) 240960

Tourist Information Centres

There are over 800 Tourist Information Centres throughout the United Kingdom and they are there for you to use both before your holiday and during it. Look in your local telephone directory under 'Tourist Information' to find your nearest centre. TIC's can give you details about local attractions, events and accommodation and many will even be able to book it for you.

Look out for the information sign.

Farming through the seasons

Agriculture is a year-round, cyclical activity. As soon as one crop is harvested, preparations get under way to grow the next. Even before Harvest Sunday is past, many farmers will have ploughed their soil and broken down the furrows by harrowing. By October disease-resistant, high-yield crops of wheat, barley and oats will have been sown. Livestock is bought and sold at fairs large and small, many of which date back centuries and have become great traditional institutions. But most farmers will be able to enjoy Christmas secure in the knowledge that their crops have been lifted, the ploughing is done and the seasonal frosts are silently crumbling the soil, letting the earth breathe and saving much hard work later.

GETTING READY

There is no break, however, in the routine of feeding and cleaning out livestock, especially now that many animals spend much of their lives indoors. Cattle, too, still need to be milked twice daily. The winer months are the time for maintenance work around the farm — repairing fences, overhauling machinery, hedging and ditching — and for poring over seed catalogues. Orders will need to be delivered early in the new year, along with fertilisers and other essentials of modern farming. In the meantime, tractors chug along country lanes, hauling manure to outlying fields ready for ploughing-in.

SOWING THE SEED

Given mild weather, sowing can begin as early as February in the southern counties. In the north — and in the south too if the winter is a bad one — it may be April before the planting season is under way. Soil compacted by winter rains is prepared by harrowing and cultivating until it is a fine and fertile tilth. As soon as the weather starts to improve, cereal crops, potatoes and vegetables of all kinds are sown, and grazing stock can go out to pasture. Spring is also the season for lambing, although some may have been born as early as Christmas. In May and June grass is cut to provide silage for winter, and later for hay, while the ceaseless work of tending the crops goes on until the first potatoes and early peas and beans are ready to be picked.

REAPING THE REWARDS

By the end of July (a month later further north) the harvest has begun in earnest: wheat, barley, oats and vegetables are brought in, and fast-growing catch crops such as rye and grass are sown for autumn grazing or winter fodder. Combine harvesters and other space-age machines become a familiar sight in the fields and on the roads as they lumber from job to job. Yet despite the hi-tech input, the farmer is still doing the same basic job that his great-grandfather did: harnessing the energy of the sun and combining it with gases in the air, moisture in the atmosphere and minerals in the soil to produce food for us all.

Further information

This is a supplementary list of workplaces full details of which were not received prior to going to press.

ENGLAND

Avon

Bath Industrial Heritage Centre
Bath
Industrial Museum

Bristol Industrial Museum
Bristol
Industry Museum

Norwood Farm
Bath
Rare Animal Breeds & Organic Cereal Growing

Bedfordshire

Gamlingay Vineyard
Sandy
Vineyard

Berkshire

Courage Shire Horse Centre
Maidenhead
Shire Horse Centre

Museum of English Rural Life
Reading
Rural Industry Museum

Buckinghamshire

Wycombe Chair Museum
High Wycombe
Chair Museum

Wickenden Vineyard
Taplow
Vineyard

The Glass Market
Wooburn Green
Glass Crafts/Works

Cambridgeshire

Duxford Airfield
Duxford
Collection of Military & Civil Aircraft

Chilford Hundred Vineyard
Linton
Vineyard

County Durham

M & M Crompton
Ireshope Burn
Craft Centre/Weavers

Cheshire

Jodrell Bank Science Centre
Lower Withington
Science Centre & Planetarium

Macclesfield Working Silk Museum
Macclesfield
Working Silk Museum & Mill

Warmingham Craft Workshops & Gallery
Sandbach
Crafts Workshop

Cleveland

Maritime Museum
Hartlepool
Maritime Museum

Cleveland Crafts Centre
Middlesbrough
Crafts Workshop

Cornwall

Helston Folk Museum
Helston
Social & Industrial Museum

Poldark Mine
Wendron
Tin Mining (Heritage)

Merlin Glass of Liskeard
Liskeard
Glass Craft

Blisland Harness Makers
Bolventor
Harness Makers

DairyLand
Newquay
Farm visitor centre

Cumbria

Penrith Steam Museum
Penrith
Working Steam Museum

Cumbria Crystal
Ulverston
Crystal Manufacturers

The Candlemakers Co Ltd
Grange-over-Sands
Candlemaking

Muncaster Mill
Ravenglass
Water-Powered Corn Mill

Pennine Tweeds
Sedbergh
Wool (Tweed) Weavers

Derbyshire

Derby Industrial Museum
Derby
Industrial Museum

Peak District Mining Museum
Matlock Bath
Lead Mining Museum

Dinting Railway Museum Centre
Glossop
Railway Museum

Andrew Lawton Furniture
Grindleford
Furniture Workshop

Weleda (UK) Limited
Ilkeston
Manufacturers of Natural Medicines & Toiletries

Caudwell's Mill Trust Ltd
Rowsley
Working Mill & Craft Centre

Devon

S Sanders & Son Ltd
Barnstaple
Sheepskin Coats ETC.

The Pixie Kiln
West Putford
Pottery Kiln Making Pixies/Gnomes

The Big Sheep
Abbotsham
Sheep Dairy Farm

The Milky Way, Downland Farm
Clovelly
Farm

Churston Pottery
Brixham
Craft Pottery

The Wheel Craft Workshops & Rest.
Chudleigh
Craft Workshops

Whitmoor House Vineyard
Ashill
Vineyard & Orchid Nursery

Dartmouth Pottery Limited
Warfleet
Pottery

J G Quicke & Partners
St Cyres
Farmers & Cheese Makers

Honiton Pottery Limited
Honiton
Pottery

Farmworld at Bodstone Barton
Combe Martin
Working Farm

Rodney Smith Woodcarving
Lydford
Woodcarving

Wood Turners Craft Centre
Modbury
Craft Centre

New World Tapestry
Mannamead
Tapestry Making

Mary Tavy Power Station
Tavistock
Power Station

Teign Valley Glass Studios & House of Marbles
Teignmouth
Glass Studio

Bickleigh Mill
Tiverton
Working Mill

The Grand Western Horseboat Co.
Tiverton
Horsedrawn Working Barges

Babbacombe Pottery
Torquay
Pottery & Tea Garden

Dorset

Broadwindsor Craft Centre
Beaminster
Craft Centre

S Moores
Morecombelake
Biscuit Bakers

Lullingstone Silk & Butterfly Farm
Sherborne
Silk & Butterfly Farm

Paws Jewellery
Bere Regis
Jewellery Craft

The Dorset Heavy Horse Centre
Verwood
Working Horse Farm

Saxon Forge
Three Legged Cross
Blacksmiths Forge

Walford Mill Craft Centre
Wimborne Minster
Craft Centre

Essex

Marsh Farm Country Park
South Woodham Ferrers
Working Farm/Country Park

Moulsham Mill
Chelmsford
Working Mill

Coggeshall Pottery
Coggeshall
Pottery

Felsted Vineyard
Felsted
Vineyard

Fullers Brickwall Farm
Sible Hedingham
Farm

Gloucestershire

St Augustines Farm
Arlingham
Working Farm & Country Centre

Summers Cider
Halmore
Cider Makers

Winchcombe Pottery
Great Winchcombe
Pottery

Whitbread Breweries
Cheltenham
Brewery

Puzzle Wood Open Iron Mines
Colford
Iron Mine

Prinknash Pottery
Cranham
Pottery

National Waterways Museum
Gloucester
Industry Museum

Three Choirs Vineyard
Newent
Vineyard

Lillian Middleston's Antique
Stow-on-The-Wold
Dolls Collection

Dennis Farm Woodware
Brimscombe
Wood Craft

Greater Manchester

Granada Television Limited
Manchester
TV Studio

Museum of Science & Industry
Manchester
Industry Museum

Hampshire

Kristen Pottery & Craft Shop
Beaulieu
Pottery & Crafts

Hollybush Farm Limited
Brockenhurst
Vineyard

Cholderton Rare Breeds Farm
Cholderton
Working Farm (Rare Breeds)

Alderholt Mill
Fordingbridge
Working Mill

Peter Ingram
Selborne
Builder, Restorer & Decorator of Gypsy Caravans

Eling Tide Mill
Totton
Tide Mill

The Pottery at Stanstead Park
Rowland's Castle
Pottery

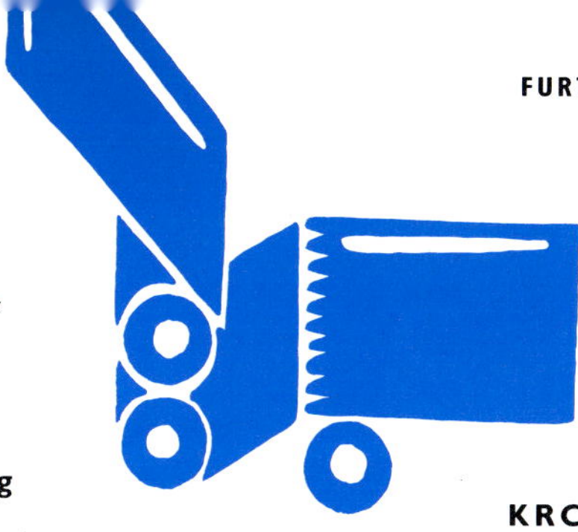

Herefordshire

Bosbury Vineyards & Gardens
Bosbury
Vineyard

Cider Museum & King Offa Cider Brandy Distillery
Hereford
Cider & Cider Brandy

Dunkertons Cider Company
Pembridge
Cider Brewery

Hertfordshire

Craft at the Malting
Meldreth
Crafts/Works

Wimpole Hall
Arrington
Farm Estate

Isle of Wight

Yafford Mill
Shorwell
Mill

Alum Bay Glass
Totland Bay
Glassworks

Isle of Wight Glass
St Lawrence
Glassworks

Kent

St Nicholas of Ash Vineyard
Ash
Vineyard

Port of Dover Tours
Dover
Port

Museum of Kent Rural Life
Sandling
Rural Industry-Heritage Museum

Hyders Limited
Plaxtol
Wrought Iron

Mill Yard Craft Centre
West Malling,
Craft Centre

Penshurst Vineyard
Penshurst
Vineyard

Whitbread Hop Farm
Beltring
Farm

Lancashire

Hand & Shuttle Crafts
Rising Bridge
Hand & Shuttle Crafts

Blackburn Lewis Textile Museum
Blackburn
Textile Industrial Museum

S & G Fowler
Arkholme
Organic Vegetables & Herbs & Goat Milk

Hornsea Potter (Lancaster)
Lancaster
Pottery

K R Cunliffes Wooden Toys & Craft
Haskayne
Wooden Toys & Craftwork

Helmshaw Textile Museum
Rossendale
Textile Industry Museum

Leicestershire

R Bass, Cabinet Maker/ Woodturner
Staunton Harold
Cabinet Maker/Woodturner

Ruddles Brewery Ltd
Oakham
Brewery

Rutland Railway Museum
Cottesmore
Railway Museum

Lincolnshire

Terry Barnatt (Glass Engraving)
Hanthorpe
Studio & Glass Engraving

Peter Tree Furniture Maker/Woodturner
Fulbeck Heath
Furniture Maker/Woodturner

Newton Newton — Flag & Banner Makers
Skegness
Heraldic Flags and Banners

London

Anthony Stern Glass Ltd
Havelock Terrace, SW8
Glass Crafts

Barbican Arts Centre
Silk Street, EC2Y
Backstage Tours

Chelsea Football Ground
Fulham Road, SW6
Football Club

Chelsea Pottery Rawnsley
Academy Ltd, Radnor Walk
SW3
Pottery

Design Museum
Butlers Wharf, SE1
Museum of Design in Mass Production

Geffrye Museum
Kingsland Road, NE2
Social & Industrial Museum

The Greyhound Brewery
Streatham Common, SW16
Independent Brewery

Kentish Town City Farm
Kentish Town, NW5
Farm

The London Glassblowing Workshop
Rotherhithe Street, E16
Glassblowing Workshop

Tottenham Hotspur Football Ground
Tottenham, N17
Football Club

London Toy Model Museum
Craven Hill, W2
Toy & Model Museum

Merseyside

Merseyside Maritime Museum
Liverpool
Maritime Museum

Middlesex

Harrow School
Harrow-on-the-Hill
Public School

Rugby Football Union
Twickenham
Sports Stadium/Rugby Union HQ

Northamptonshire

Stencil Interiors Craft Workshop
Harringworth
Craft Workshop

The Copper Gallery
Desborough
Designs and Forge

Norfolk

Norfolk Shire Horse Centre
West Runton
Shire Horse Centre

North Elmham Winery & Vineyard
North Elmham
Vineyard

The Particular Pottery & Gallery
Kenninghall
Pottery

Lexham Hall Vineyard & Winery
Litcham
Vineyard

Norfolk Lavender Ltd
Heacham
Lavender Farm

Tony Clements
Terrington St Clement
Horticultural Centre

Bridewell Museum of Local Industries
Norwich
Industry Museum

City of Norwich Craft/ Design Ctr.
Norwich
Craft & Design Centre

Tom Smith Crackers
Norwich
Cracker Manufacturing

Holkham Pottery Ltd
Wells next Sea
Pottery

Northumberland

Allenheads Heritage Centre
Allenheads
Craft/Industrial Heritage

Errol Hut Smithy/ Woodwork
Cornhill-on-Tweed
Smithy/Woodwork Craft Centre

Lindisfarne Limited
Holy Island
Winery

D.G. Burleigh
Longframlington
Northumbrian Pipe Makers

Chantry Silver
Morpeth
Silver Works

Northumbria Centre
Morpeth
Craft Centre

Nottinghamshire

Chris Aston Pottery
Elkesley
Pottery

Dolly Mixtures
Old Bilsthorpe
Antique Porcelain Dolls/ Victoriana/Pottery

Rufford Craft Centre
Ollerton
Crafts Centre

Nottinghamshire Cricket Club
Nottingham
Test Cricket Ground

Nottingham Woollaton Industrial Museum
Woollaton Park
Industry Museum

Longdale Rural Craft Centre
Ravenshead
Rural Craft Centre

Oxfordshire

Bothy Vineyard
Frilford Heath
Vineyard

The Old School Jewellery & Silversmithing Workshop
Wantage
Jewellery & Silversmith Workshop

Shropshire

Acton Scott Working Farm
Nr Church
Working Farm Museum

Pastoral Crafts
Melverley
Pastoral Crafts

Somerset

Moorlynch Vineyard
Bridgwater
Vineyard

Quantock Weavers
Over Stowey
Weavers

Castle Cary Vineyard
Castle Cary
Vineyard

Hornsbury Mill
Near Chard
Historical (Working) Mill

Somerset Rural Life Museum
Chilkwell Street
Rural Industry/Heritage Museum

Perrys Cider Mill
Dowlish Wake
Cider Mill

Chewton Dairy Farms Limited
Mendip
Dairy Farm

Little Creech Domestic Animal Centre
West Hatch
RSPCA Animal Centre

Willow & Wetland Visitor Centre
Stoke St Gregory
Willow Craft Industry

Wookey Hole Caves Limited
Wells
Hand-Made Paper Makers

Staffordshire

Piano Workshop
Newborough
Piano Workshop

Ceramadad Pottery
Leek
Pottery

Royal Park Hall China Ltd
Longton
China Manufacturer

Suffolk

Cavendish Manor Vineyards
Cavendish
Vineyard

Ostler Dairy Flock
Horringer
Dairy Farm

Lowestoft Fishing Industry
Lowestoft
Fishing Industry Working Tour

Bruisyard Vineyards
Saxmundham
Vineyard & Herb Garden

Further information continued

Surrey

Studio/Furniture Workshops
Cranleigh
Craft Workshops

Horton Park Farm
Epsom
Farm

Redgrave Theatre
Farnham
Theatre Tour

Loseley Park
Guildford
Farm & Dairy

Merrist Wood College of Agriculture & Horticulture
Worplesdon
Agricultural & Horticultural College

Sussex

Amberley Chalk Pits Museum
Nr Arundel
Social/Industrial Museum

English Wine Centre
Alfriston
Vineyard

Jill Pryke Pottery
Ditchling
Pottery & Sussex Crafts Centre

The Truggery
Herstmonceux
Established Trug Makers

Barkham Manor Vineyards
Piltdown
Vineyard

Sussex Highweald Dairy Sheep
Duddleswell
Sheep Dairy Farm

Jacques Ruijterman
Arundel
Fine Glass — Craft

Geraldine St. Aubyn Hubbard
Nutbourne
Craft Shop

Burstye Soays
Lindfield
Specialist Soay (Rare Breed) Sheep

Washbrooks Farm Centre
Hurstpierpoint
Working Farm Centre

Coombes Farm Tours
Lancing
Working Farm

Tyne & Wear

Museum of Science & Engineering
Newcastle-upon-Tyne
Industrial Museum

Vaux Breweries Ltd
Sunderland
Brewery

Warwickshire

Middleway Clocks & Furniture
Shenton
Restoration/Antiques

Wiltshire

Wilton Windmill
Nr Marlborough
Working Windmill

West Midlands

Museum of Science & Industry
Birmingham
Industry Museum

The Black Country Museum
Dudley
Industrial Heritage Museum

The Lock Museum
Willenhall
Industrial Heritage Museum

Worcestershire

Jinney Ring Craft Centre
Hanbury
Crafts Centre

Annard Woollen Mill
Church Lench
Woollen Mill

R A Rogers "The Basketmaker"
South Littleton
Basket Making

Rajcol Dairy Products Ltd
Worcester
Dairy Farm

Yorkshire

Crakehall Water Mill
Bedale
Water Mill

Village Craft Centre
Hunmanby
Crafts Centre

W R Outhwaite & Son (Rope makers)
Hawes
Rope Makers

Mohair Producers Ltd
Wykeham
Mohair/Yarn Producers & Suppliers

John Smiths Ltd
Tadcaster
Brewery

Lister & Co at Bingley Mills
Bingley
Working Mills (Silk Manufacturing)

South Square Centre
Bradford West
Craft Workshops

Bradford Industrial Museum
Bradford
Industry Museum

Leeds Industrial Museum
Leeds
Industry Museum

Booth House Gallery
Holmfirth
Art & Craft Gallery

Calderdale Industrial Museum
Halifax
Industry Museum

Horses at Work
Halifax
Working Horses

SCOTLAND

Aberdeenshire

Russell Gurney Weavers
Muiresk Turriff
Handloom Weavers

Dee Valley Confectioners
Ballater
Confectionery Manufacturers

James Cocker & Sons
Lang Stracht
Rose-Fields & Suppliers

Jennie Ross Knitwear
near Ellon
Knitwear Manufacture

Campmill Village Trust
Bieldside
Various home crafts

J I Crichton
Braemar
Woodcraft

Grampian TV
Aberdeen
TV Studios

Angus

Oathlaw Pottery
By Forfar
Pottery

Rudeigin Beag
Backmuir of Liff
Dolls Houses & accessories

Angus Handloom Weavers
By Montrose
Handloom Weaving

The McIntosh Rocking Horse
By Montrose
Manufacture of Rocking Horses

Argyll

Campbeltown Creamery Limited
Campbeltown
Cheese Manufacture

Inverawe Smokehouses
Taynuilt
Smoking of Fish & Game

Kath Small
Ballachulish
Craftmade Jewellery

Kilmartin Crafts
Kilmartin
Wood Turning

Ayrshire

Dalgarven Mill — The Living Past Museum
Kilwinning
Bread & Home Baking — Restored Flour Mill

Banffshire

Portsoy Marble Company
Portsoy
Marble & domestic pottery

Berwickshire

The Homestead Pottery
Coldstream
Pottery

Liz Rowley (Stained Glass)
By Lauder
Stained glass work

Water Lily Weavers
Coldstream
Handweaving for the interior

Caithness

Caithness Candles
John O'Groats
Candle design makers

Dunlin Designs
Murkle
Hand Puppets & Patchwork

Milton Gallery
Lyth
Furniture making & Wood Turning

Dumfrieshire

Gracefield Arts Centre
Dumfries
Ceramics, Porcelain

Esk Cottage Studio
Langholm
Pyrography Art Photography & Sculpture in wood

East Lothian

Shape Scape Ceramics
North Berwick
Pottery, Ceramics

Glassworks
Musselburgh
Studio Glassmaking

L'Argenette
North Berwick
Jewellery Manufacture & Design

Fifeshire

Crail Pottery
Crail
Pottery

Margaret Oliver Pottery
North Queensferry
Pottery

The Pottery Workshop
St Andrews
Pottery and Porcelain

St Andrew's Fine Bone China
St Andrews
Manufacture of Fine Bone China

Houses of Scotland
St Andrews
Design of card cut-out models

Ready Set Sew
Falkland
Patchwork/Quilting Workshop

Inverness-shire

Culloden Pottery
Gollanfield
Pottery

Rothiemurchus Estate
by Aviemore
Cattle, Deer & Trout farming, Forestry & Conservation

Highland Pottery
Newtonmore
Pottery

Lynda Usher
Invermoriston
Hand-knitted knitwear

Veronica Togneri Weaving Studio
Culloden Moor
Distinctive Handwoven Woollen Rugs

Mike Crummy — Tomatin Smithy
Tomatin
Design & Making hand forged decorative metalwork

Isles

Silverbirch Spinning & Weaving Workshop
Whiting Bay, Isle of Arran
Handspinning & Weaving

Isle of Bute Pottery Ltd
Rothesay, Isle of Bute
Pottery

Dabbles
Kilchattan Bay, Isle of Bute
Spinning/weaving/knitting

Fear an Eich — Coll Pottery
Back, Isle of Lewis
Pottery, Ceramics

Nesstex
Ness, Isle of Lewis
Harris Tweed & Spartan Weaving

Blett Studio/Eday Spinners
Calf Sound, Isle of Eday
Handspinning & Water Colour

Judith Glue
Kirkwall, Orkney
Knitwear/Watercolour artist

Lindoor Sheepskins
Rendall, Orkney
Tanning Sheepskin Rugs

Barbara Isbister
Cunningsburgh, Shetland
Knitwear

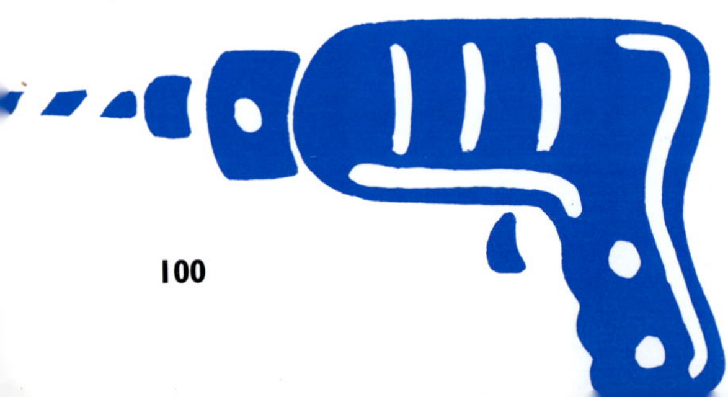

L J Smith & Shetland Woollen Co
Scalloway, Shetland
Knitwear Manufacture

Oxensetter Originals
Ollaberry, Shetland
Knitting & Dress Making

Edinbane Pottery
Edinbane, Isle of Skye
Pottery

Hebridean Crofts Originals
Loch Boisdace, Isle of South Uist
Hand-framed knitwear

Lanarkshire

Springburn Museum
Glasgow
Social & Industry Museum

Midlothian

Scottish Hydro-Electric Plc
Edinburgh
Power Station

Fountain Brewery
Edinburgh
Brewery

Royal Mile Living Craft Centre
Edinburgh
Crafts Centre

McDonalds Muir Ltd
Leith
Distilleries

Christian Shaw Stained Glass
Edinburgh
Stained Glass

Mark Powell
Edinburgh
Precious Metals Craft

Castlecliff Workshop
Edinburgh
Craft Workshop

Morayshire

Tugnat Ice House
Moray, Scotland
Salmon Fishing Industry

Moray Old Mills
Elgin
Working Mill

Baxters of Speyside Ltd
Fochabers
Foods

Darnaway Farm Visitor Centre
Darnaway
Farm Centre

Peebleshire

Traquair House Brewery
Innerleithen
Brewery

Ross-shire

Glenelg Candles
Glenelg
Candle Maker

Foxfarm Weaving Workshop
Ardross
Weavers

Lochcarron Weavers
Lochcarron
Weavers

Roxburghshire

Kelso Pottery
Kelso
Pottery

Wrights of Trowmill Ltd
Hawick
Weavers

Derek Irvin (Furniture)
Mossburnford
Furniture Workshop

Creetown Gem Rock Museum
By Newton Stewart
Gem Jewellery Workshop

Stirlingshire

Glengoyne Highland
Dumgoyne
Whisky Distillers

Barbara Davidson Pottery
Larbert
Pottery

Sutherlandshire

Far North Pottery
Durness
Pottery

MacKenzie-Harris Leathercraft
Bonar Bridge
Leather Bag Manufacturer

Orcadian Stone Company Ltd
Golspie
Gem Stones & Jewellery

Please check opening times and admission fees (if any) in advance wherever possible.

WALES

Clwyd

Llangollen Weavers
Llangollen
Woollen Weavers

Ruthin Craft Centre
Ruthin
Craft Centre

Sharp Manufacturing Company
Wrexham
Electrical/Electronic Equip. Man.

Shotton Paper Company
Shotton
Paper Mill

Dyserth Hand Weavers
Dyserth
Cloth Weaving

Dyfed

Brynonen Farm
Whitland
On-Farm Goat Milk Cheesemaking

John M Price & Son
Talsarn
Forge

Llywernog Silver Lead Mine Museum
Ponterwyd
Silver Lead Mine Museum

Stoney Park Weavers
Narbeth
Weavers

Tregwynt Woollen Mill
Letterston
Woollen Mill

Wallis Woollen Mill
Haverfordwest
Woollen Mill

Glamorgan

DB Stoneware
Pontypridd
Stoneware Pottery

Ewenny Pottery
Near Bridgend
Pottery

Hoover plc
Abercanaid
Manufacturers/Domestic Appliances

Natural Beauty Products
Bridgend
Cosmetics

S A Brain & Co Ltd
Cardiff
Brewery

Welsh Industrial & Maritime Museum
Cardiff
Industrial & Maritime Museum

Gwent

Pells Quality Confectionery Ltd
Newport
Quality Confectionery

Bigpit Mining Museum
Blaenavon
Mining/Colliery Works

Silurian Ceramic Crafts
Pontllanfraith
Ceramic Craft Works

Tintern Parva Vineyard
Tintern
Vineyard

Gwynedd

Dolwyddelan Pottery
Dolwyddelan
Pottery

Penmachno Woollen Mill
Nr Betws-y-Coed
Woollen Mill

Porthmadog Pottery
Snowdon Street
Pottery

Powys

The Benson Group
Knighton
Heavy Equipment

Corris Craft Centre
Machynlleth
Craft Centre

National Centre for Alternative Technology
Machynlleth
Alternative Technology

Welsh Royal Crystal
Rhayader
Crystal Glass

Maritime & Industrial Museum
Swansea
Maritime & Industrial Museum

Factory shops

In addition to visiting workplaces it is possible to purchase many products in shops at the place of manufacture —you will find many listed in this Guide. Look out in bookshops in many parts of the country for the Factory Shop Guide series of publications which give full details.

Tourist Boards

National Tourist Boards

English Tourist Board
Thames Tower, Black's Road,
Hammersmith,
London W8 9EL
081-846 9000

Scottish Tourist Board
23 Ravelston Terrace,
Edinburgh EH4 3EU
031-332 2433

Wales Tourist Board
Brunel House, 2 Fitzalan
Road, Cardiff CF2 1UY
(0222) 499909

Northern Ireland Tourist Board
River House, 48 High Street,
Belfast BT1 2DS
(0232) 231221/246609

England's Regional Tourist Boards

Cumbria Tourist Board
Ashleigh, Holly Road,
Windermere, Cumbria
LA23 2AQ.
☎ (096 62) 4444.

East Anglia Tourist Board
Toppesfield Hall, Hadleigh,
Suffolk IP7 5DN.
☎ (0473) 822922.

East Midlands Tourist Board
Exchequergate, Lincoln 2 1PZ.
☎ (0522) 531521.

Heart of England Tourist Board
Woodside, Larkhill,
Worcester WR5 2EQ.
☎ (0905) 613132.

London Tourist Board
26 Grosvenor Gardens,
London SW1W 0DU.
☎ 071-730 3450.

North West Tourist Board
The Last Drop Village,
Bromley Cross, Bolton,
Lancashire BL7 9PZ.
☎ (0204) 591511.

Northumbria Tourist Board
Aykley Heads, Durham
DH1 5UX.
☎ 091-384 6905.

South East England Tourist Board
1 Warwick Park, Tunbridge
Wells, Kent TN2 5TA.
☎ (089 25) 40766.

Southern Tourist Board
40 Chamberlayne Road,
Eastleigh, Hampshire
SO5 5JH.
☎ (0703) 620006.

Thames & Chilterns Tourist Board
The Mount House, Church
Green, Witney, Oxon.
OX8 6DZ.
☎ (0993) 778800.

West Country Tourist Board
Trinity Court,
27 Southernhay East,
Exeter EX1 1QS.
☎ (0392) 76351.

Yorkshire & Humberside Tourist Board
312 Tadcaster Road,
York YO2 2HF.
☎ (0904) 707961.

Questionnaire

Future editions of this guide and other tourist publications are being planned for the future. If you would like details please complete below your name and address including your postcode:

____

____

____

____

____

____

Your comments and suggestions regarding this guide would also be appreciated either criticism or constructive ideas and information.

____

____

____

____

____

____

____

Further copies should be obtainable from your book shop. Otherwise send a cheque for £2.95 (payable to Visitor Publications Limited) with your name and address to Visitor Publications Limited, Surrey House, Surrey Street, Croydon, Surrey CR0 1SZ. ☎ 01-681 2696. Fax 01-688 5550.

Questionnaire

Future editions of this guide and other tourist publications are being planned for the future. If you would like details please complete below your name and address including your postcode :

Your comments and suggestions regarding this guide would also be appreciated either criticism or constructive ideas and information.

Further copies should be obtainable from your book shop. Otherwise send a cheque for £2.95 (payable to Visitor Publications Limited) with your name and address to Visitor Publications Limited, Surrey House, Surrey Street, Croydon, Surrey CR0 1SZ. ☎ 01-681 2696. Fax 01-688 5550.

Questionnaire

Future editions of this guide and other tourist publications are being planned for the future. If you would like details please complete below your name and address including your postcode:

____

____

____

____

____

____

Your comments and suggestions regarding this guide would also be appreciated either criticism or constructive ideas and information.

____

____

____

____

____

____

____

Further copies should be obtainable from your book shop. Otherwise send a cheque for £2.95 (payable to Visitor Publications Limited) with your name and address to Visitor Publications Limited, Surrey House, Surrey Street, Croydon, Surrey CR0 1SZ. ☎ 01-681 2696. Fax 01-688 5550.

Questionnaire

Future editions of this guide and other tourist publications are being planned for the future. If you would like details please complete below your name and address including your postcode :

____

____

____

____

____

____

Your comments and suggestions regarding this guide would also be appreciated either criticism or constructive ideas and information.

____

____

____

____

____

____

____

Further copies should be obtainable from your book shop. Otherwise send a cheque for £2.95 (payable to Visitor Publications Limited) with your name and address to Visitor Publications Limited, Surrey House, Surrey Street, Croydon, Surrey CR0 1SZ. ☎ 01-681 2696. Fax 01-688 5550.

Tourist Information Centres

There are over 800 Tourist Information Centres throughout the United Kingdom and they are there for you to use both before your holiday and during it. Look in your local telephone directory under 'Tourist Information' to find your nearest centre. TIC's can give you details about local attractions, events and accommodation and many will even be able to book it for you.

Look out for the information sign.

Visitor Publications Limited

is part of a group of companies including:
James of Fleet Street Limited
The Perfect Design Company Limited
Financial & Industrial Publicity Services Limited
Independent Media Services Limited

Surrey House, Surrey Street
Croydon, Surrey CR0 1SZ
☎ 01-681 2696. Fax 01-688 5550

INDEX OF ADVERTISERS

Index of advertisers

Page numbers of display advertisements are shown in blue.

A

Abbeydale Industrial Hamlet **57**

Allied Distillers Ltd **71**

B

Bass Mitchells & Butlers Ltd **55**

Bass Museum, Visitor Centre & Shire Horse Stables **47**

Belleek Pottery Ltd **88**, **89**

Berkeley Power Stn (Nuclear Electric) **32**, **11**

Boosey & Hawkes Musical Instruments Ltd **44**

Boscastle Pottery **23**

Bosham Walk Craft Ctr **54**

Bradwell Nuclear Power Stn (Nuclear Electric) **32**, **11**

British Nuclear Fuels plc (Sellafield) **27**, **16**

Bulmer Brick & Tile Co Ltd **53**

Bunnahabhain Distillery **64**

C H Brannam Ltd **29**

C

Cadbury World **55**, **IFC**

Caithness Crystal Ltd (King's Lynn) **45**

Caithness Glass plc (Wick) **66**

Caithness Glass plc (Perth) **70**

Callestock Cider Farm **23**

The Cambrian Factory **81**

Carnforth Railway Restoration & Engineering Services **40**

Cheddleton Flint Mill **50**

Chessell Pottery (IOW) Ltd **35**

Coldharbour Mill **29**

Colonial Candle Co Ltd **27**

Coloroll Edinburgh Crystal **67**

Coronation Rock Co Ltd **39**

Culloden Pottery **66**

Cumberland Pencil Museum & Exhibition Centre **26**

D

Dartington Crystal **29**

David Evans & Company **38**

Dean Heritage Centre **32**

Deep Sea Adventure **30**

Denby Pottery Visitor Ctr **28**

Dinorwig Pumped Storage Power Station **81**

Dounreay **65**, **11**

Dungeness Power Station (Nuclear Electric) **39**, **11**

E

Easton Farm Park **53**

Eldridge Pope & Co plc **30**

ECC International Ltd **26**

Etruria Industrial Museum **50**

Eurotunnel Exhibition Centre **38**, **IBC**

F

Farm & Country Visits **54**

Ffestiniog Pumped-Storage Power Station **79**

Finch Foundry & Museum of Waterpower **30**

Fleet Air Arm Museum **47**

Frederic Robinson Ltd **22**

G

Geevor Tin Mines & Museum **23**

Glenturret Distillery Ltd **69**

Gloddfa Ganol Slate Mine **79**

Goonhilly Satellite Earth Station **23**

H

Hartlepool Nuclear Power Stn (Nuclear Electric) **22, 11**

Harts Silversmiths **33**

Harveys Wine Museum **20**

Hebridean Jewellery **71**

Heysham Power Stn (Nuclear Electric) **40, 11**

Heredities Ltd **26**

Highland China Ltd **66**

Highland Tryst Museum **70**

Highland Wineries **66**

Hinkley Point Power Station (Nuclear Electric) **46, 11**

Hornsea Pottery **57**

House of Hardy Ltd **45**

I

Inigo Jones & Co Ltd **80**

J

J Ellis & Sons (Bordon) Ltd **34**

James Johnston & Company of Elgin Ltd **68**

James White Suffolk Cider **52**

John Hine Ltd **34**

John Ridley Projects Ltd **69**

John Taylor Bellfoundry & Museum **41**

John Walker & Son **65**

John Wood & Sons (Exmoor) Ltd **47**

K

Kelham Island Industrial Museum **57**

L

Lathkill Dale Craft Ctr **27**

Lamberhurst Vineyards **39**

Lambourn Trainers Association **20**

Llechwedd Slate Caverns **79**

Lloyd's of London **41**

The London Diamond Ctr **42**

London Docklands Development Corporation **42, 13**

Longdown Dairy Farm **34**

Lower City Mills **70**

M

Massey-Ferguson Tractors Ltd **55**

Maude Walkley Cloggs **57**

Maxwell Hemmens Precision Steam Models **58**

Meon Valley Vineyard **34**

Merrydown Wine plc **55**

N

Nevern Dairies Ltd **78**

Newmarket Equine Tours **53**

Norfolk Rural Life Museum **45**

Norselands Gallery Studio 2 **46**

North Wootton Vineyard **47**

Northern Ireland Tourist Board **89**

Nuclear Electric (see Berkeley, Bradwell, Dungeness, Hartlepool, Heysham, Hinkley Point, Oldbury, Sizewell, Trawsfynydd, Wylfa)

O

Oban Glassworks **64**

The 'Old Bushmills' Distillery Company Ltd **88, 89**

continued on next page

INDEX OF ADVERTISERS

Index of advertisers cont

Editorial management, design, production, advertisement sales, distribution & published by: Visitor Publications Limited

Editorial: Tim Shackleton

Line entry compilation: Janet Smith

Typesetting: Em Photosetting

Printed in Great Britain by Grove Web Offset Limited

Photography: Britain on View Picture Library; p3 Quarry Bank Mill, Royal Doulton; p4 Easton Park Farm; p5 British Nuclear Fuels, Wootton Vineyard; p6 David Evans; p7 Wootton Vineyard; p17 Wedgwood, Cheddleton Flint Mill; p18 Telecom Showcase; p19 David Evans; p25 Eldridge Pope; p28 Stevenson Bros; p36 Wootton Vineyard; p37 Wootton Vineyard; p40 Wedgwood; p46 Eldridge Pope; p48 Wedgwood; p61 Highland Tryst Museum; p62 The Mill Shop; p75 and p76 Inigo Jones; p77 Ffestiniog Power Station; p79 Culloden Pottery; p80 Longdown Dairy Farm; p82 British Nuclear Fuels; p83 Telecom Showcase; p85 Culloden Pottery; p90 Longdown Dairy Farm; p110 Telecom Showcase;

Surrey House, Surrey Street, Croydon, Surrey CR0 1SZ
☎ 01-681 2696

ISBN 0-9515831-0-7

O

Oldbury Nuclear Power Stn (Nuclear Electric) **20, 11**

Otterton Mill Ltd **29**

P

Park Lodge Farm Centre **44**

Pembroke Power Station **78**

Porridge Press Printers **69**

Port Sunlight Heritage Ctr **44**

Powergen **56, 12**

Priory Vineyards **31**

Q

Quarry Bank Mill **22, 59**

Quince Honey Farm **30**

R

Redesdale Dairy **46**

Redman & Hales Ltd **31**

Ridgeway Cottage Industry Centre **28**

Royal Brierley Crystal **56**

Royal Doulton **50**

Royal Grafton China **51**

Royal Worcester Ltd **35**

S

Sacrewell Farm & Country Centre **21**

Scotch Whisky Heritage Centre **68**

Scotherbs **69**

Scottish Mining Museum **68**

Scottish Power (Cruachan Power Station) **64**

Shire Horse Trust & Carriage Museum **26**

Sizewell Information Centre (Nuclear Electric) **53, 11**

Spode **51**

South Leaze Sheep Farm **56**

Staffordshire Enamels Ltd **51**

Stevenson Brothers Rocking Horse Gallery & Workshop **38**

Stockwood Craft Museum **20**

Stott Park Bobbin Mill **27**

Summerlee Heritage Trust **67**

T

Tattenhall Dairy Products Ltd **21**

Telecom Technology Showcase **42**

Thames Barrier Visitors Ctr **43**

The Thames Valley Vineyard **21**

Thursley Textile Designs **54**

Tilbec **33**

Tower Bridge **43**

Trawsfynydd Power Station (Nuclear Electric) **80, 11**

Treske Ltd **58**

Tutbury Crystal Glass Ltd **50**

Tyrone Crystal **88, 89**

W

Walsall Leather Centre Museum **56, 59**

Warburtons Ltd **40**

Wedgwood Visitor Ctr **51, 14**

Whitbread Beer Company **78**

Whitbread & Company plc (Hartlepool) **22**

Whitbread & Company plc (Lancashire) **41**

Whitchurch Silk Mill **35**

William Grant & Sons Ltd **65**

The Wimbledon Lawn Tennis Museum **43**

The Working Silk Museum **31**

Winter Flora Ltd **52**

Wylfa Power Station (Nuclear Electric) **80, 11**

Y

Yorkshire Mining Museum **58**

For details of advertising opportunities contact:
Advertisement Dept, Visitor Publications Limited, Surrey House, Surrey Street Croydon, Surrey CR0 1SZ
☎ 01-681 2696